# GRISWOLDVILLE

# GRISWOLDVILLE

*The Story of the Industrial Village
Founded in Central Georgia by Samuel Griswold,
Its Antebellum Prosperity and Role in the War Effort
of the Confederate States of America,
and Its Destruction during the March to the Sea,
together with Accounts of the Military Operations
Conducted in Griswoldville's Vicinity
during the Summer and Fall of 1864*

William Harris Bragg

MERCER UNIVERSITY PRESS
MACON, GEORGIA
2000

MUP/ P396

© 2009 Mercer University Press
1400 Coleman Avenue
Macon, Georgia 31207

First Paperback Edition.

Original Hardback Edition published in 2000.

Book design by Burt&Burt

Books published by Mercer University Press are printed on acid free paper that meets the requirements of American National Standard for Information Sciences— Permanence of Paper for Printed Library Materials.

Mercer University Press is a member of Green Press initiative (greenpressinitiative.org), a nonprofit organization working to help publishers and printers increase their use of recycled paper and decrease their use of fiber derived from endangered forests. This book is printed on recycled paper.

*Library of Congress Cataloging-in-Publication Data*

Bragg, William Harris.
    Griswoldville / William Harris Bragg.—1st ed.
    p. cm.
    ISBN 13: 978-0-88146-168-8
    1. Griswoldville (Ga.), Battle of, 1864. 2. Griswoldville (Ga.)—History—19th century. 3. Griswoldville (Ga.)—Social Conditions—19th century. I. Title.

E477.4.B73 2000
973.7'37—dc21                                             99-05884

# IN MEMORIAM

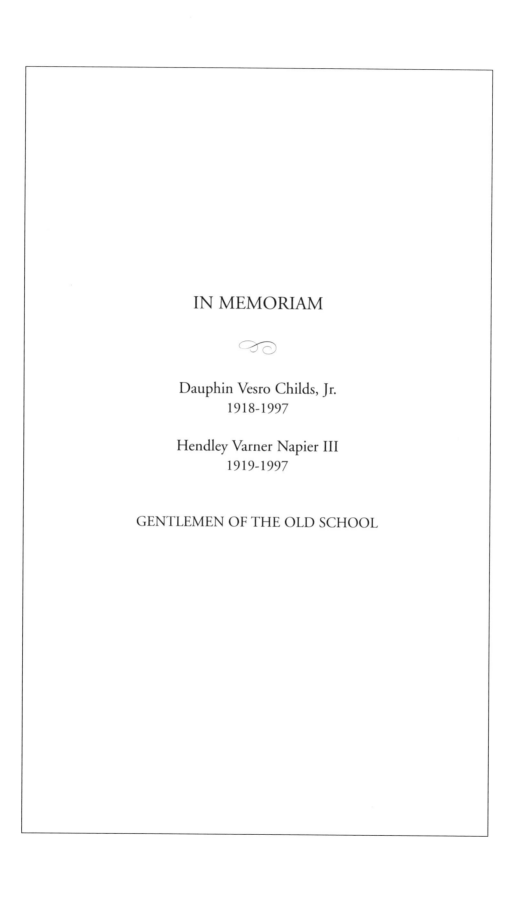

Dauphin Vesro Childs, Jr.
1918-1997

Hendley Varner Napier III
1919-1997

GENTLEMEN OF THE OLD SCHOOL

Detail of the Edward Forbes etching "Going into Camp at Night." (Courtesy of the Dover Pictorial Archives Series.)

# Contents

Samuel Griswold, c. 1860. Like many of the antebellum South's industrialists, Griswold was a native Northerner who later became an ardent Confederate. (Courtesy of Laura Nelle O'Callaghan.)

# Introduction

For such a small battle, Griswoldville has always attracted great interest, particularly from those drawn to the story of the Civil War in Georgia. But those with broader concerns have also felt its appeal, notably Shelby Foote, who wrote affectingly of the battle in the last volume of his Civil War trilogy.

In numerical terms the battle was practically negligible: more Federals were counted missing after the fighting at Chickamauga (around 4700), than fought on both sides at Griswoldville (fewer than 4000). But what the battle lacked in size and scope was more than made up for in terms of human interest: no mention of the battle ever seems to neglect a reference to the old men and young boys of the Georgia Militia and their ill-starred charge against seasoned, entrenched Union troops. Also, the battle undeniably has a claim to uniqueness, as the only major infantry engagement of the March to the Sea. Beyond that there is the link to what Griswoldville had meant before that raw November day in 1864: the location of a remarkable and justly famed Confederate pistol factory. And the factory's previous incarnation as a center for cotton gin production nicely illustrates the "ploughshares into swords" aspect of Southern military industrialization.

The following pages attempt to touch briefly on all such aspects of the story of Griswoldville, as village (in peace and war) and as battlefield (in both Stoneman's Raid and Sherman's March). Since there would have been no Griswoldville without Samuel Griswold, it seemed fitting to begin and end the story with him. The account of his life, enterprises, and village forms a thread that runs throughout the narrative. Nonetheless, that thread occasionally disappears as it interweaves with descriptions of those momentous events of the war's last year that were to alter forever Griswold and all his creations.

At the risk of "loitering on the threshold" of a book, as Charles Dickens termed it, I wish to add a final comment on *Griswoldville*'s illustrations: they aim both to complement and supplement the narrative, and their captions often contain information not found in the text.

The "Brick House," Clinton. Here the Griswolds rented rooms during their early days in Georgia; in later years it formed part of Samuel Griswold's vast property holdings. (Georgia Department of Archives and History.)

# 1.
# THE RISE OF SAMUEL GRISWOLD

In 1815—with the second war with England ended and the Indian threat less menacing—thousands of immigrants began moving into the newly peaceful border lands of the southeastern United States. Among them came Samuel Griswold, twenty-six, of Connecticut, with his wife, Louisa, and two infant children. Like a number of Virginians and Carolinians before them, the Griswolds settled in the central Georgia village of Clinton, seat of Jones County.[1]

Clinton, founded a few years earlier, sat between the Ocmulgee and Oconee Rivers in what had been Creek Indian territory until 1804. The Ocmulgee, fifteen miles west of Clinton, marked the end of the region open to white settlement. Near its banks—in a Federal reserve carved from Jones County's southwestern corner—stood the rough stockade and twin blockhouses of Fort Hawkins. Two other outposts—Forts Pinckney and Early—guarded the more northwesterly river crossings into the Creek lands. Twenty miles east of Clinton, on the west bank of the Oconee, lay Milledgeville, Georgia's capital since 1804. Despite its towering Gothic state house, the capital city was itself little more than a frontier town.[2]

On Samuel Griswold's arrival in Clinton, the village still contained some cabins, but there were also several frame structures—like the houses of Roger McCarthy and Captain Jonathan Parrish. Also, plans were well underway for a stately brick courthouse that would be completed in 1818. The village was growing rapidly. Its 1810 population of eighty-five would increase almost tenfold by 1820, the year that a massive three-story brick building, known as the "Brick House," was completed near the court-house. For a time Griswold and his family would occupy rooms on the building's second floor, with mercantile shops below and the meeting rooms of the Freemasons above.[3]

As Clinton grew, Samuel Griswold prospered, and his family increased by six children. Though Griswold began as a mere clerk for one of Clinton's merchants (with his wife doing seamstress work), he was soon self-employed as a tin-ware dealer, selling articles he produced. By 1820 he was able to buy a dwelling house and two town lots in Clinton, as well as five slaves. But his initial success with buckets and baking pans proved short-lived. In the early 1820s came a serious reversal of fortune, apparently linked to security debts. In any case, he was forced to borrow money from a Connecticut lender and to sell his town property.[4]

Before long, however, a fortunate visit to the plantation of Thomas Blount, two miles south of Clinton, led Griswold toward remarkable prosperity. Blount had recently purchased a cotton gin, and upon examining it, Griswold decided that he could build one that was equal or better. He was correct. With little capital, he rented a blacksmith shop. There, using simple tools and assisted only by his eldest son, Griswold began manufacturing sturdy, uncomplicated gins. By early 1825, he had purchased the smithy lot and adjacent property and was rapidly expanding his enterprise, adding machinery and operatives. By the late 1820s, Griswold's newspaper advertisements offered excellent terms to prospective purchasers—gins, "superior to any in use," that the manufacturer would deliver at a modest charge and would take back at his own expense, with a refund, if any gin was not "a good one."[5]

With cotton king of the Southeast, and machines for processing it in high demand, Griswold soon expanded his operations again. In 1830 he bought over 400 acres on the southwestern edge of Clinton on the road to Macon, a village that had sprung up across the Ocmulgee from Fort Hawkins. Below the Macon road Griswold built a spacious gin factory, along with an iron foundry, smithies, and other shops, including one for making carriages. And on the hill across the road from his business, Griswold built a "beautiful residence" of two stories that faced Clinton. Soon his establishment became "the largest producer of cotton gins in the nation," as his long, mule-drawn wagons hauled his products to buyers throughout Georgia and the Carolinas.[6]

Griswold did not manufacture a spike gin like the Eli Whitney original. Instead, he produced a saw gin like the machine designed by Whitney's rival, South Carolinian Henry Ogden Holmes. Though some of Griswold's earliest gins were evidently of the smaller, hand-cranked variety, most of his later models were much larger and could be powered

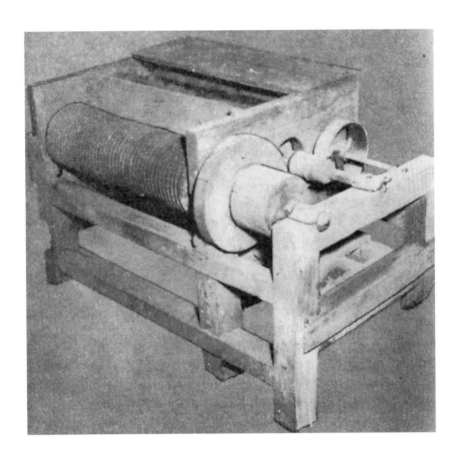

A Griswold cotton gin. This model, which was powered by water, is now owned by the Old Clinton Historical Society. (From James C. Bonner's *The Georgia Story* [1958].)

# DIRECTIONS FOR USING YOUR GIN.

The band should be six inches wide after it is stretched, out of well tanned, even thickness, pliant harness or belt leather. A Gin cannot run light without a wide band of suitable leather.

The Gin should set level on the floor, the long way, the ends perpendicular by a plumb line, bearing equally on each leg or post; one side may be higher than the other, if necessary, but if one end is higher than the Gin an inch or more on blocks, the seed will incline to the low end and break the roll.

You will discover an idle pulley, or whirl, in a small frame, not made fast to the Gin, which use as follows: if the band runs through the back side of the Gin, as is most common, let the pulley and frame remain as it is, both parts of the band running above the pulley, the under part bearing on it, and as the band stretches, shove up the frame to tighten it; but if the band comes out in front of the Gin, which is sometimes the case, then take out the frame and pulley, and place in front, near the Gin and the floor, for both parts of the band to run under, the upper part bearing against the pulley, so as to wrap as much as possible around the pulley on the saw shaft.

Close up tight the back side of the Gin, from the moat or flue-board down to the floor.

If you wish all the moats taken out, raise or shove out the moat-board as far as it will allow and not drop too much lint with the moats, and turn up the buttons at the lower corners to hold it; by having the moat-board so high as to drop two or three pounds of lint with the moats during the ginning, each bag will gain in quality four times the loss in quantity.

If the seed are not well cleaned, raise the tail of the breast and turn up the buttons placed below, and let the breast rest on them; or if it picks too slow with the breast raised, perhaps by raising the front of the Gin an inch or more on blocks, the breast may be let down again. The seed of damp cotton are more difficult to clean than dry—it may require the breast or Gin raised for damp cotton, and allowed to be down for dry. Some seed shed better than others, some incline to lodge on the breast, and not fall freely, in that case raise the back side of the Gin one inch, or more if required. Raising the tail of the breast will prevent cotton napping, unless very much too damp, and will make the quality of any cotton better, because it gins slower; and especially when ginning Mastodon, the tail should be raised more or less, according to the condition of the cotton and fineness of the saw teeth; if necessary for either, the tail of the breast may be raised as high as it will allow and keep the roll in operation, by adding to the thickness of the buttons with wood or leather. Cotton should, however, be dry, if possible, when ginned; no fast Gin can gin damp cotton without napping more or less.

Run the brush band over the brush pulley; if the band becomes too slack, cut out about one inch and a half, and fasten as before—if it needs cutting again, shorten it not more than one inch: neither band should be tighter than absolutely necessary to keep their place and the Gin running; too tight a band causes the boxes to heat and wear out much faster, and the draught to be much more heavy on the team.

It is well to use a bushel of cleaned seed, mixed with seed cotton, at the first start.

While feeding a Gin, the Ginner should be constantly putting cotton into the box with the fingers, in small quantities, regular from end to end, rather the most at the ends, as fast, and no faster than the seed can be cleaned and discharged; if fed too fast, too many seed will accumulate in the box, and break the roll; if too slow, the seed will shed foul; either will retard the progress and lessen the quantity ginned. Should the roll break from over-feeding, slacken the feed, and shake the box by raising and lowering at the tail, instead of using a stick. If the roll breaks when the Gin is regularly fed, you may know one end of the Gin wants raising more or less.

Keep the boxes constantly oiled with lamp oil or soft grease—tallow is better than nothing, but must be pressed down very often, or it will not settle down within reach of the gudgeon. I send a can extra, to induce you to use lamp oil—the gudgeons should not run a moment without being covered with grease of some kind.

Your cotton or lint room should be as long and high as possible, and so wide as not to obstruct the passage of the lint after it leaves the brush. If it is on the floor with the Gin, as is most common, it should be closed tight all round, top, bottom, sides and ends, except one opening of about two feet wide, at the back end of the floor over head, a little more or less, just sufficient to let out the wind made by the brush, which will create a draught through the room, and send the cotton much of it to the far end before it falls, which will open the lint, and sample better, than if dropped near the Gin; besides, it prevents the lint from dropping under the Gin, which is frequently the case when the lint room is out of order. This draught may be further assisted by having a door or window through the wall, directly in front of the Gin; if a window, it should extend to the floor. If too much lint should fall under the Gin, you may know it is for want of a draught, which may be remedied as above directed: if the lint falls into a room below, that also should be tight. No doors or windows allowed to be open when ginning.

If the saws rub the breast, first ascertain on which side, then move the whole in the opposite direction, with the screw in the box at that end of the cylinder, first turning back the screw in the opposite end, as much as the other requires turning forward; and be particular not to turn either too much—a thickness of paper may be sufficient,—merely start the screw as little as possible, and try until it runs clear; and be certain not to let both press against the ends of the cylinder, allow them to touch so slight as only to keep the cylinder in place, and not bind in the least. A wrench is sent with the Gin, for turning the screws.

The team should not be drove faster than a brisk walk while ginning, and should be made gentle before starting a new Gin; brushes are frequently broken by fractious teams—all sudden starts should be avoided.

The inside of the Gin should be cleared of lint once or more each day, and if the cotton is damp, the saw teeth should be cleaned at night after work, and wiped dry with cotton. Great care should be taken to keep out sticks, rocks, nails, &c.

A Gin cannot pick fast with a slow gear, nor run light with one badly made, nor perform well and keep in order, without proper attention and good treatment. All cast gear within my knowledge, run slow and pull heavy.

My Gins are proven to perform well before leaving the factory, and if the above directions are followed, I warrant them to do so, on trial by the purchasers.

**SAMUEL GRISWOLD.**

*Clinton Geo. May 18 1848.*

*Wm. R. Enochs. Esq*
*By the bearer I send you one 40 Saw Gin with castile plata ribs as ordered by Lewis Parker Esq which I hope may reach you safe and give full satisfaction, enclosed you have a blank note for $90. which you may sign and send by the bearer, the same may be paid Jany next with eighty dollars*
*Yours Respectfully*
*Samuel Griswold*

---

Purchasers of Griswold gins were provided with a sheet of detailed directions. On this specimen Griswold appended a signed note. (Hargrett Rare Book and Manuscript Library, University of Georgia Libraries, Athens, Georgia.)

by horse or mule, water or steam. Most gins had approximately forty circular, axle-mounted saws whose teeth passed through narrow ribs to pull away the lint from the cotton bolls, leaving the seeds behind. Horse-powered gins sometimes used as many as sixty saws, and water-powered ones as many as eighty. Griswold even filled one order for a 105-saw gin, for an "eccentric planter" who had heard that no existing gin had more than one-hundred saws.[7]

Hard work and good business sense had carried Griswold far, but he also chose wisely in selecting colleagues to help him improve his product. From Connecticut came the Brown brothers, Israel and Dwight, extremely proficient mechanics who would later make names for themselves in manufacturing gins and other agricultural machinery. The Browns created a variety of machines that punched out parts for assembly into superior gins, using the finest English steel from the Naylor works in Sheffield.[8]

In the early 1830s Griswold formed another valuable alliance with Daniel Pratt, formerly of New Hampshire. During a decade in central Georgia, Pratt had won distinction as a gifted carpenter-architect, and was responsible for the most handsome residence in Clinton, Lowther Hall. Pratt's carpentry skills no doubt helped perfect the wooden framing and cabinets of the Griswold gin stands, and he moved quickly from factory foreman to partner. But Pratt soon decided to continue westward and struck out for Alabama, hauling with him several wagon-loads of disassembled Griswold cotton gins. Increasingly successful, Pratt became a leading manufacturer and distributor of gins in his own right, surpassing Griswold to become the producer of "the most popular gins in the South." Alabama's first major industrialist, Pratt had by 1838 centered his various factories and shops in his own community, Prattville, just northwest of Montgomery.[9]

Throughout the 1830s and 1840s Griswold continued to expand his various enterprises and to accumulate more property, including the "Brick House," where in less prosperous days his family had rented rooms. By 1849, he was selling eight hundred gins per season and was expanding into Cherokee Georgia, the northwestern section of the state. There, in Rome, planters from upcountry Georgia and northeastern Alabama could

Daniel Pratt in old age. Once Griswold's employee, he eventually surpassed him as an industrialist. (From Mrs. S. F. H. Tarrant's *Hon. Daniel Pratt: A Biography* [1904].)

buy Griswold gins from a branch of the firm known as Griswold & King. By this time the gins were not only "warranted to perform well," but were "delivered free of expense to the purchaser." In an advertisement, Griswold noted that because of "long experience, first class mechanics, best materials, and the most improved machinery," he was able to offer "an article, which, for faithful workmanship, durability, and superior performance" was unsurpassed by any in the country. His new, improved gins, he added, included "Reid's Patent Combination Box," and he had also "procured at great cost the sole right to use on Cotton Gins Devalin Wood and Hancock's celebrated Oil-Saving Box," unexcelled by "any now in use."[10]

## 2.
## A HANDSOME AND THRIFTY VILLAGE

Unlike Daniel Pratt, who at Prattville harnessed the swift waters of Autauga Creek, Griswold had no source of water power in Clinton and ran his operations with steam. He also appreciated the importance of steam power to transportation and saw the great potential of the Central of Georgia Railroad, chartered in 1833 to link coastal Savannah with the now-burgeoning young town of Macon. Consequently, Griswold in the mid-1830s began purchasing land in the southern portion of Jones County, on and near the railroad's path. Though he was among those who contracted to prepare part of the line's roadbed, he valued his thickly wooded acreage more as a source of lumber for his Clinton factories. With the railroad's completion in 1843, Griswold's land purchases along the line increased and included a parcel on the headwaters of Swift Creek with a "primitive" water-powered saw mill. But by 1850 he had erected a modern steam saw mill at a site on the railroad. Griswold then decided to go

Daniel Pratt one better by doing what the Alabama industrialist would never do: move his establishment to a rail line.[11]

Thus was born Griswoldville, ten miles south of Clinton and nine rail miles east of Macon. Griswold's workmen fed pine logs into his saw mill and took out the planking to build numerous structures. Soon a gin factory rose, with its tall brick chimney and several satellite buildings (such as long sheds for storing and seasoning lumber). Also constructed were a grist mill, blacksmith and pattern shops, a soap and tallow factory, and a foundry. Numerous cottages sprang up as well, for both Griswold's white operatives and for his slaves. The latter numbered ninety-one by 1850 and would increase to 108 over the next decade. Griswold also built houses for some of his children and in-laws, and, for the creator of Griswoldville himself, "a fine three-storied family residence of twenty rooms, [with] outhouses, laundry, large barns, and stables." The mistress of the house, now far from the days when she worked as a seamstress in Clinton, had her own sewing machine, the first in the county. And the mansion's well-stocked library more than met the family's voracious reading tastes.[12]

Residents of the village, both white and black (for the slave mechanics were paid wages), patronized Griswold's general store, whose stock equaled most such emporiums. Trains delivered all manner of goods from numerous sources, including fresh oysters from Savannah, almost two hundred miles distant by train. There was also a post office (with Samuel Griswold as postmaster) and a non-denominational church, where various ministers preached on alternate Sundays. When a "hard-shell Baptist preacher" accused Griswoldville Church of being only for "Methodists and rich folks," Griswold responded without anger. "I have built a church here," he said; "it doesn't belong to the Methodists but to me. The Methodists have one Sunday in the month in which to use it, but you can have one if you want it. I would be glad for you to use it; my folks are all Methodists, but damned if I ain't sorter Baptist."[13]

As Station Number Eighteen on the Central railroad, Griswoldville also had a depot, water tank, wood rack, and a lengthy siding north of the main track. Passengers on the road viewed the industrial village (the last station before Macon) with much interest. Wrote one young lady in 1852,

Lowther Hall, Clinton, a masterpiece of Daniel Pratt. (Georgia Department of Archives and History.)

"The prettiest town on the [Central railroad] is Griswoldville.... The streets are wide and straight and planted with trees.... and it promises to become a flourishing place." The next year a column in the *Southern Recorder* in Milledgeville gave another description: "The observant traveler upon the Central Railroad is not a little surprised, soon after leaving Macon, to come upon a handsome and thrifty little village, lying in ambush among tall graceful pines. This oasis in the desert has been brought into prosperous being by the indomitable and well-directed energy and perseverance of one man. If others would imitate his laudable example, our 'pine barrens' would soon teem with a thrifty and valuable population." A correspondent of the *Savannah Courier* concurred: "Everything [about Griswoldville] convinces you that [Samuel Griswold] *is a business man.* Neatness and order are to be seen in every direction. The manufacture of cotton gins [is] the business of the village, and Mr. G. has acquired a celebrity in this line unequaled by any other gentleman in the State."[14]

The census statistics for 1850 confirmed Griswold's success. He was by then selling annually 900 gins ("worth not less than $40,000"), as well as $80,000 worth of gin saws. His enterprise was consuming, each year, some "70,000 pounds of castings, mostly of iron," as well as "50,000 pounds of wrought iron, 40,000 pounds gin-saw cast steel, and 200,000 feet of lumber," though his saw mills actually produced three times that amount.[15]

By 1860, Griswold enjoyed even greater prosperity, with real and personal property totaling well over a quarter million dollars. His land purchases had made him owner of most of southwest Jones County, and possessor of much acreage in adjacent Twiggs County as well—over 11,000 acres total. Taking the train from Griswoldville to Macon, Griswold passed through no land in Jones County that was not his. By this point, with his children grown and married, he was now also allied with several of the other prominent families of the county, including the Johnsons, the Hardemans, and the Bonners. Richard Wyatt Bonner and his wife, Griswold's daughter Ellen, now lived in the old Griswold house on the edge of Clinton. Across from it, several of the family businesses still

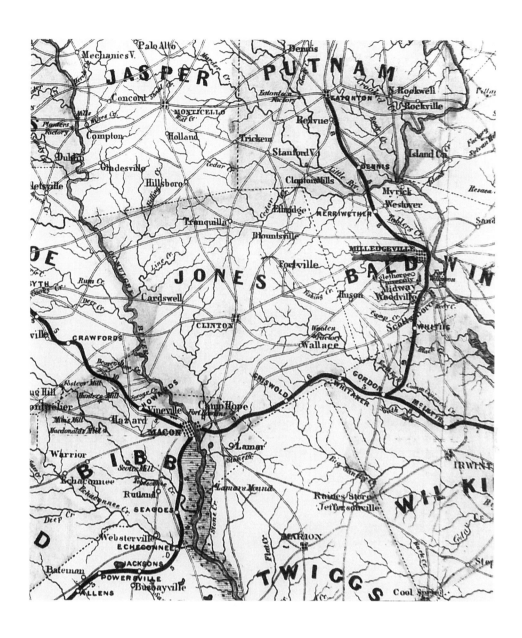

Confederate Middle Georgia. This detail of *Lloyd's Topographical Map of Georgia* (1864) shows most towns and villages but only the major thoroughfares. (Hargrett Rare Book and Manuscript Library, University of Georgia Libraries.)

A Griswold pike head. At the base of the central blade only the last several letters of Griswold's name are legible, the product of imperfect stamping. (Virginia Historical Society, Richmond, Virginia.)

operated, including "wagon and buggy factories and a farm implements factory."[16]

But, just as Macon had replaced Clinton as the principal town of Middle Georgia, Griswoldville by 1860 rivaled Clinton as the busiest town in Jones County. Clinton's population had by then dwindled to around 300 people, just as Jones County itself was down to around 9,000—a sad decline from the 1820 population of over 16,000, which Macon and Bibb County had now finally reached. Though half Clinton's size, Griswoldville had become a popular destination for planters, farmers, and others, whether they wanted to catch the train or ship freight (from peaches to cotton), to bring corn or wheat to be ground, or to take away everything from scantlings to barrels of fertilizer. Likewise, with houses of worship popular as places of both spiritual renewal and socializing, Griswoldville Church was often well-attended by worshippers from far afield.[17]

### 3.
### WEAPONS FOR THE WAR

Though the coming of war in 1861 found Samuel Griswold extremely prosperous, he no longer enjoyed good health. During the late 1850s circulatory problems had led to a debilitating stroke. Increasingly moody, Griswold had all but retired from business affairs, now left mainly to his son Giles, who also oversaw the family's farming operations. When the war failed to end as quickly and successfully as predicted, Griswold's principal enterprise—gin manufacturing—became outmoded. In the fields of the South cotton would have to give way to food and forage crops, and agricultural machinery would be much less needed than weaponry. Griswold determined to adapt.[18]

As a first step, Griswold's factory quickly answered Georgia governor Joseph E. Brown's call for the production of pikes for the war effort. Brown was certain that pikes would prove to be effective, inexpensive weapons to arm those Southern soldiers who could not be equipped with rifles. The spear-like weapons were considered excellent arms for infantry to use against cavalry, though this idea—like that of using pikes in general—worked better in theory than in practice.[19]

The Griswold pike was of the three-bladed cloverleaf variety. Its large central blade, ten inches long, was flanked, just above the socket, by two 3-inch blades projecting at right angles. The head itself was mounted on a tapered wooden shaft, six or seven feet long, with a knobbed butt. Within a two-month period beginning in April 1862, Griswold shipped 804 pikes to the state armory in Milledgeville. So that there would be no confusion over who had produced these polearms (and who would be paid the $4020 that this work grossed), the pike heads were stamped "S. Griswold."[20]

Unlike Prattville, with its Prattville Dragoons, Griswoldville would produce no namesake company of Confederate fighting men. But several Southern units would become familiar with Samuel Griswold's industrial village. Centrally located on a major rail artery, Griswoldville served well as a site for mustering Confederate and state troops, who were also allowed to camp and train in the nearby fields. Among the camps established there were Camp Griswold, used by the Thirtieth Georgia Regiment in the winter of 1861-1862 (during which time Griswold supplied the men with meal and beef), and Camp Wayne, where the Second Regiment, Georgia State Line, was organized in the spring of 1863. As the war dragged on, other soldiers were brought to Griswoldville, not for training but for treatment at the Confederate hospital located there. From his shops, Griswold furnished the hospital with two of its major necessities: beds and coffins. And his village's Georgia Chemical Factory supplied castor oil, an increasingly rare medication. The Confederate Medical Examining Board also met in Griswoldville to examine conscripts as well as sick and wounded soldiers.[21]

Arvin Nye Gunnison (1825-1882). After a career that took him from New Hampshire to Louisiana and Georgia, Gunnison retired to Mississippi and died in the town that bears his name. (Gunnison Library, Gunnison, Mississippi.)

A Griswold & Gunnison revolver, Serial Number 3530. (The Museum of the Confederacy, Richmond, Virginia. Photography by Katherine Wetzel.)

Among Georgia's soldiers in Confederate service were several of Griswold's grandsons, one of them his namesake in the Macon Volunteers, Samuel Griswold Johnson, son of Francis S. Johnson and Griswold's daughter Lucia. Young Sam Johnson had been raised in his parents' house on Madison Street in Clinton, opposite the site where his grandfather had made his start in gin manufacturing. The spacious Johnson residence, though plain in exterior, was famed for having a particularly sumptuous parlor where French wallpaper—depicting a garden scene—extended "entirely around the walls, like an immense tapestry."[22]

Sam Johnson's letters from the Virginia front made it clear that, though the country was beautiful, comforts were scarce. Then, in May 1863, the young man was seriously wounded at Chancellorsville and sent back disabled to Clinton. A few weeks later, seemingly much improved, Johnson made an awkward jump from a buggy at church. Jolted into a fatal hemorrhage of his wound, he died in mid-June 1863.[23]

By that time Samuel Griswold had lost to death all but two of his eight children, including his three sons. When Griswold's last surviving son, Giles, had died unexpectedly in May 1862, plans were well underway for a second venture into providing weaponry for the embattled South. This time, however, the Griswold factory would produce not pikes but six-shooter percussion-cap pistols patterned after the celebrated .36 caliber Colt Navy Revolver, a favorite—especially of cavalrymen—for over a decade. Since the Confederate government had by this time chosen Macon as one of its major military-industrial centers, Griswoldville was as well placed for providing pistols to the Confederacy as it had been for producing polearms for the state of Georgia.[24]

Griswold's son-in-law and attorney, E. C. Grier, would prove a very valuable employee of the new pistol works. But the firm would be known as Griswold & Gunnison, since Griswold's co-owner was a business associate of long standing, Arvin Nye Gunnison, originally from New Hampshire. From the mid-1850s Gunnison had occupied a position of trust in the gin manufacturing operation at Griswoldville. He had later moved to New Orleans, where he manufactured his own line of gins as part of the firm of Gunnison, Chapman & Company. By early 1862

Gunnison had also made a start in manufacturing revolvers, but, with the fall of New Orleans in April of that year, he had returned to Griswoldville, bringing with him some machinery and his "indispensable" factory foreman.[25]

In contracting with the Confederate government in May 1862 for the production of pistols, Griswold & Gunnison hoped eventually to be able to produce "fifty to sixty pistols per week," at a price of $40 per weapon. By mid-July, the firm had twenty-two machines in operation. But Walter C. Hodgkins, the superintendent of the Armory Department of Macon's Confederate Arsenal, saw room for improvement in the newly-organized Griswoldville pistol works and expressed doubts about some of the procedures in practice. Nonetheless, the revolvers soon proved able to pass his "severe" tests.[26]

The *Macon Telegraph* quickly trumpeted Griswold & Gunnison's success in an editorial of August 5, 1862:

> We were equally surprised and gratified…at the sight of a Colt's Navy Repeater, made at the machine shop…at Griswoldville…. The weapon had just passed the inspection of the Confederate Superintendent of Armories…, and a contract had been made…. The pistol, to our inexperienced eye, was as well finished as those made by the patentee himself, and we have no doubt equally efficient….
>
> The specimen before us was the first fruit of the skill and inventive ingenuity in elaborating machinery and tools for the purpose, of men who had never seen a pistol shop, or a single tool or piece of machinery for making them. The machines now in use have all been contrived and built since last March, and the force of the establishment diverted from the manufacture of Cotton Gins to the making of Colt's revolvers. With the well known resources and enterprise of this concern, we need not say the business under their hands will grow to meet any demand upon them. —This is a strong illustration of the power of the South to supply her own wants. We certainly had no idea that a manufactory of Colt's pistols would spring up near Macon in 1862.[27]

Major General George Stoneman, USA. His military career would have its share of disasters; in postwar politics he would be elevated to the California governor's chair. (Library of Congress.)

Two previously unpublished wartime views of General Stoneman: Cartes-de-visite from the studio of Alexander Gardner, Washington, DC. (Courtesy of David Wynn Vaughan.)

Though not as refined a piece of workmanship as the Colt on which it was patterned, the Griswold & Gunnison pistol was a handsome and serviceable sidearm. Part of its attractive appearance was due to the Confederacy's scarcity of needed materials. Steel for framing was hard to come to by and iron proved unsuitable, so the Griswoldville Confederate Colt was framed in gleaming brass, some of it from bells donated by churches in Macon and elsewhere. The contrast between the dull sheen of the ironwork, the glowing brass frame and foresight, and the grained walnut grips produced a very distinctive appearance. In action, the Griswold & Gunnison revolver proved dependably lethal.[28]

A curious aspect of the revolvers' production was noted by Superintendent Hodgkins in one of his first reports: the machines at the pistol factory were worked by "twenty four hands—twenty two of whom [were] Negro Slaves." This number increased in time, and the slaves obviously took great pride in their work and appeared to see no irony in producing weapons to be used against those who might seek to liberate them. This, at least, seems to be the subtext of a newspaper account of a brief visit to southern Jones County in late October 1863 by Jefferson Davis: "At Griswoldville, on the Central Railroad, where the President arrived between eight and nine o'clock on Friday night, about forty Negroes, laborers in Mr. Griswold's pistol shops at that place, had collected and manifested great anxiety to see Mr. Davis. Being told of it, he got off the car and went the rounds, taking each one by the hand and giving him a pleasant word."[29]

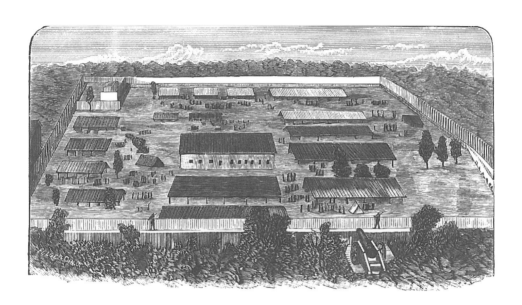

Macon's Camp Oglethorpe Prison. "The prison grounds were square," recorded one of Camp Oglethorpe's inmates, "and included an area of nearly three acres, inclosed by a tight board fence about twelve feet high.... The daily ration per man consisted of one pint of corn meal; a quarter of a pound of bacon; one ounce of rice; one ounce of dried beans; and one teaspoonful of salt." (From Asa B. Isham et al., *Prisoners of War and Military Prisons* [1890].)

Colonel Horace Capron, USA. Born in 1804, Capron was better known as a "progressive farmer" than as a soldier. During the Stoneman Raid he was distracted by the presence of his seventeen-year-old son, whom he feared would be captured and sent to Andersonville. (US Army Military History Institute, Carlisle Barracks, Pennsylvania.)

Colonel James Biddle, USA. At the Battle of Sunshine Church, Biddle assisted in covering the escape of most of the Yankee raiders and then helped persuade Stoneman to surrender. (US Army Military History Institute.)

Colonel Silas Adams, USA. Colonel Adams's Unionist Kentuckians helped themselves to the bounty they discovered south of Atlanta. But one of his officers worried that "thieving expeditions never thrive." (From Eastham Tarrant's *The Wild Riders of the First Kentucky Cavalry* [1894].)

4.
# SABERS IN CENTRAL GEORGIA

By the time Davis visited Griswoldville, Confederate hopes had declined dramatically with the disasters at Gettysburg and Vicksburg the previous summer. More than ever, men were needed for the Confederate armies, but those involved with the Griswoldville pistol works were recognized as too necessary to the war effort to be subject to either conscription or active militia duty. According to Special Orders, No. 95, for example—issued on 1 August 1863, by Georgia Adjutant and Inspector General, Henry C. Wayne—Samuel Griswold, A. N. Gunnison, and seven others, including E. C. Grier, were to be allowed to "remain at their posts of labor." It was noted, however, that they were nonetheless expected to "[attach] themselves to the nearest company of Confederate or State employees organized for local defense."[30]

Local defense had assumed increasing importance in Georgia by late 1863, for two great armies of the Union and Confederacy were then locked in a struggle for Chattanooga, Tennessee. That town's permanent loss to the Confederacy by year's end left Georgia open to an invasion by Union forces. Griswoldville, though continuing to produce revolvers with admirable regularity, was beginning to seem much less the secure rural backwater than it had in the past.[31]

In the spring of 1864, when the Union and Confederate forces began their "red clay minuet" toward Atlanta, Griswoldville became even more vulnerable, partially because of its proximity to Macon, which ranked high on the list of Union targets. Macon had become one of the Confederacy's most important centers for producing war materiel—the site of foundries and rifle and sword factories, as well as an armory, arsenal, and ordnance laboratory. The city also hosted branches of the central government's treasury, quartermaster, and commissary departments. By the time Major General William T. Sherman began encircling Atlanta, Macon had become a hospital center as well, filled with the human wreckage of the long campaign.[32]

As crucial as were these local and national considerations to Macon's importance, another of the town's Confederate facilities put Macon—and, consequently, Griswoldville—on the itinerary of Major General George Stoneman, one of Sherman's cavalry commanders. In the last sweltering days of July 1864, Stoneman determined to take Macon and break open the town's Camp Oglethorpe prison to free the Yankee officers held there.[33]

Located at Macon's southern edge near the rail yards, Camp Oglethorpe's timber stockade enclosed approximately fourteen-hundred Union officers, who were housed in spartan frame barracks. But Camp Oglethorpe was not Stoneman's primary target. It lay further south: Camp Sumter. This sprawling, unroofed prison for Federal enlisted men was located in the hamlet of Andersonville, which gave the facility the name by which it was most widely known, feared, and reviled. The savior of Andersonville's thirty-thousand overcrowded and suffering prisoners would surely win all the love and laurels that a grateful North could bestow.[34]

Stoneman could use the glory. A forty-two-year-old West Pointer from New York, he had risen rapidly during the war's first year, ultimately taking charge of the cavalry of the Army of the Potomac. But failures in 1863's Chancellorsville Campaign had lost him the trust of his superiors and had pushed him on an even faster downward spiral. After medical leave (ingloriously, for hemorrhoids), Stoneman was exiled to General William T. Sherman's army in the Tennessee-Georgia theater. Now, Stoneman hoped, a successful raid into central Georgia would bring him not only fame and glory, but much-needed rehabilitation for his reputation as well.[35]

Unfortunately, Stoneman's questionable fitness for such a daring enterprise was matched by the dubious qualities of some of the officers and many men in the three brigades under him. His brigadiers ranged from the elderly agriculturist Horace Capron (distracted by the presence of his teenage trooper son) to the Kentucky Unionist Silas Adams, who ranked self-preservation high among his goals. Only Brigadier General James Biddle seemed unquestionably adequate to the task confronting Stoneman and his raiders. Likewise, Stoneman's men—even by the noto-

Captain William A. Lord, USA. One of Stoneman's staff officers, he frequently led Capron's brigade during the fighting below Hillsboro. (From W. L. Sanford's *History of the Fourteenth Illinois Cavalry* [1898].)

Lieutenant Lewis W. Boren, USA. A member of Major Francis Davidson's detachment, Boren helped destroy Gordon and the Oconee railroad bridge. (From W. L. Sanford's *History of the Fourteenth Illinois Cavalry* [1898].)

riously casual standards of the cavalry arm—were dangerously undisciplined. This fatal laxness was particularly conspicuous among Silas Adams's Kentucky cavalrymen, who were nearing completion of their enlistment. Stragglers without peer, they often allowed personal whim to override lawful orders.[36]

Stoneman's plan to liberate the Yankee prisoners in central Georgia would have taxed his force enough under any circumstances. But, according to Stoneman's orders, the Macon-Andersonville raid was merely an addition to a more important movement. Sherman, preparing to mount what he hoped would be the final infantry assault of the Atlanta Campaign, had directed Stoneman—with some 2000 troopers and a battery section equipped with two Rodman guns—to unite below Atlanta with another cavalry force, commanded by Brigadier General Edward M. McCook. These forces were directed to destroy a considerable portion of the Macon and Western Railroad near Lovejoy's Station, after which Stoneman would be free to embark on his central Georgia raid. With luck, Sherman's campaign would soon end, with Atlanta captured and the Union prisoners freed.[37]

Stoneman began well enough. Leaving camp near Decatur with his raiders on the morning of 27 July 1864, he proceeded cautiously, leaving behind at Flat Rock a cavalry division under Brigadier General Kenner Garrard to confuse and delay any pursuing Confederate horsemen. But, by the next morning, Stoneman's men found that plunging into previously untouched Rebel territory was a heady experience, particularly so for the Kentuckians. They began the raid by becoming riotously drunk in Covington, soon after the raid began, and one of their officers, Captain Frank Wolford, committed murder by shooting down a citizen in the streets. After a fruitless search for bridges to take them west to Lovejoy's Station, Stoneman and his men abandoned McCook and proceeded toward Macon via Monticello and Clinton. Though rapid movement was now crucial, the raiders moved slowly, delayed by looting and burning along the way. They also ran off numerous horses and mules along their path and found willing slaves to drive them. These bondsmen, soon joined by others thirsting for freedom, grew to such numbers that one Federal officer called them the "Negro Brigade." On a practical level, these "contrabands" were a serious impediment and another cause of delay.[38]

A Bird's Eye View of Clinton in the Mid-1800s.

Based upon art work by Orran L. Hudson that appeared in *Old Clinton Historic Preservation Plan* (1976). An evocative but somewhat fanciful reconstruction, it nonetheless gives a good basic view of the town's plan and major structures. The surrounding countryside, however, would have been mostly cleared and under cultivation. [Numbers and identifications added]. (Middle Georgia Regional Development Center, Macon, Georgia.)

*(Asterisks mark existing structures.)*

* 1. The Jones-Ross House
* 2. Clinton Methodist Church
  3. Clinton Baptist Church
  4. The Griswold-Bonner House
  5. The Griswold-Gin Factory
  6. Griswold's First Gin Shop
  7. The Hamilton-Johnson House
* 8. The Clower-Gaultney House
* 9. The Jones House
  10. the Brick House

# CLINTON

# 5.
# STONEMAN'S RAIDERS AT CLINTON AND GORDON

At about noon on Friday, 29 July, the lead elements of Stoneman's force clattered across the Bray Creek bridge north of Clinton and rode without resistance into the town. Citizens eating their midday meals suddenly heard cries of "The Yankees are coming!" and found the road leading toward Griswoldville and Marion clogged with dust-coated Federal horsemen. Seven-year-old William Wiley Barron had a perfect vantage point for witnessing the excitement. His father's home, a rambling former hotel called the "Old Castle," stood at the corner of Madison Street and the Marion road. Stoneman, "wearing a tremendous black hat," impressed the boy as "a fine looking man, …very tall with broad shoulders." On asking directions to Macon, however, Stoneman heard bad news from Barron's father: the bridge to Macon (and Camp Oglethorpe) had recently washed away.[39]

Though Stoneman and most of his mile-long column cleared Clinton without delay, some raiders stayed behind to loot in earnest and were soon enthusiastically joined by stragglers. Newspaper reports would estimate that losses to thievery and destruction during Stoneman's raid amounted to over a half million dollars in Jones County alone, mainly in Clinton and on the nearby plantations of the Blounts, the Bowens, and the Barrons. One journalist declared that Stoneman's "conduct in Jones County was such as to merit the most ignominious death."[40]

Though stolen and runaway slaves perhaps made up a significant (and presumably temporary) percentage of the monetary losses cited, thefts of jewelry, money, clothing, brandies and wines, and livestock were considerable. The raiders, according to one report, "entered private houses and stripped ladies of rings and pins; broke open drawers and trunks, stole silver and plate of every description." At Lowther Hall, a party of raiders forced the venerable Elizabeth Lowther "to deal out wine in the wine cellar, whole crowds of them standing by and threatening death if they were not served next." Oddly, the remaining Griswold enterprises at Clinton

Major General Howell Cobb, CSA. The wealthy owner of several plantations, Cobb was one of the most estimable men in Georgia and the Confederacy, having been governor of his state, a US congressman, a member of James Buchanan's cabinet, and chairman of the Montgomery Convention. (Hargrett Rare Book and Manuscript Library, University of Georgia Libraries.)

The "Bear's Den," Howell Cobb's residence on Walnut Street in Macon. Its distinctive name—which suited Cobb—was given the house by its former owner, Cobb's bachelor brother-in-law John B. Lamar, mortally wounded at Crampton's Gap in 1862. In the "Bear's Den," Cobb played host to numerous Confederate generals and statesmen—including P. G. T. Beauregard and Jefferson Davis. (Library of Congress.)

appear to have been untouched, though the nearby Bonner home, Samuel Griswold's former residence, was among the many pillaged.[41]

In one instance north of Clinton, the raiders' depredations were not suffered helplessly. Just above Hillsboro lived elderly John McKissick, famous for his fiery temper. He did what many middle Georgians doubtless wanted to do. When some raiders rode into his yard, he took his shotgun and blew one of the Yankees out of the saddle. Summarily, he was borne off from his screaming wife, who was assured by the raiders that her husband would be hanged at their earliest opportunity.[42]

Upon leaving Clinton, Stoneman divided his forces and sent them in several directions. Adams and his Kentuckians were sent toward Macon on the direct road, where they were delayed all afternoon and most of the night by a detachment of cavalry from Macon. Stoneman, accompanying Biddle's and Capron's brigades, marched toward bivouac on the Garrison Road, a thoroughfare south of Clinton that connected Macon and Milledgeville. Earlier a 125-man force under Major Francis Davidson had been sent southeast to wreck the rail junction at Gordon and prevent any reinforcements from being sent by train from Milledgeville. At Gordon, Davidson's men did considerable damage, destroying several trains and torching several buildings. They then rode east and delivered an even heavier blow by burning the great railroad trestle over the Oconee River. It would take almost a month (and installation of a Howe truss bridge) to restore regular rail communication between Macon and Savannah.[43]

# 6.
# COBB'S RESERVES AND BROWN'S "PETS"

Meanwhile, Macon had been warned by telegraph of Stoneman's foray the day the raiders left camp, and a small army had gathered there, contrary to Stoneman's hopes. Macon was now headquarters of Major General Howell Cobb, the portly commander of Georgia's Confederate Reserve Force and a more than usually effective "political general." An aristocratic planter from Athens who had served as Georgia's governor and as treasury secretary in President James Buchanan's administration, Cobb had his Reserve headquarters on Mulberry Street but conducted much of his business at his nearby residence, a mansion near the west bank of the river known as the "Bear's Den." There he often played host to Confederate luminaries, including President Jefferson Davis, of whom he was a staunch ally.[44]

In fact, Cobb's presence in middle Georgia was designed to help Davis counterbalance the anti-administration activities of Governor Joe Brown, who for some time had been engaged in a tug-of-war with Richmond over Georgia's dwindling manpower resources. Brown considered the only constitutional means of raising troops in the Confederacy to be through volunteering and through requisitions on the governors as commanders-in-chief of the militia. These methods had created the Confederate armies of 1861-1862, to which Georgia had contributed heavily. The governor detested the conscription acts; they had ended the requisition system and had tried to draft all of Brown's available militia between seventeen and fifty. But, despite conscription legislation, the governor had by early 1864 enrolled almost 25,000 ostensibly exempt Georgians from that coveted seventeen-fifty age group, which he called the "Militia Proper." The rigors of the third conscription act of February 1864 had taken most of these men from Brown, while giving boys between seventeen and eighteen and men between forty-five and fifty to General Cobb to organize into a Confederate local defense force. Much like the state militiamen, Cobb's soldiers were normally to be called up only during emergencies.[45]

Joseph E. Brown, War Governor of Georgia. The title of this piece of sheet music, published in Macon, would have an ironic aspect after the events of November and December 1864. But Brown's was certainly an imperial governorship, particularly in the eyes of the Richmond administration. (Hargrett Rare Book and Manuscript Library, University of Georgia Libraries.)

Henry C. Wayne, Adjutant & Inspector General of Georgia. Responsible for all of Georgia's state troops, Wayne also commanded the First Division, Georgia Militia, until the election of Gustavus Woodson Smith could be arranged by the governor. (Georgia Historical Society, Savannah, Georgia.)

Major General Gustavus Woodson Smith, Georgia Militia. A former Confederate general (and fervent anti-Davis man), Smith led the First Division, Georgia Militia, during the last year of the war. (From Francis T. Miller's *The Photographic History of the Civil War* [1911].)

Theoretically, Brown was left with only his "Militia Reserve," boys sixteen and seventeen and men between fifty and sixty, numbering some 16,000. But Brown would organize them around and through his "Pets," state civil and militia officers whom he shielded from conscription through exemptions, and whose numbers he increased with numerous appointments. Consequently, there would be considerable numbers of conscription-age militiamen. As Cobb tried to enlist Georgians in the Confederate Reserve Force, Brown hampered him whenever possible and organized the Militia Reserve and conscription-age exempts into his last state army: the First Division, Georgia Militia. This organization was well-described by Robert Toombs, who as its inspector general and chief of staff was tasked with making it battle-ready. It was "a mixed crowd," he noted, "a large number of earnest, brave, true men; then all the shirks and skulks in Georgia trying to get from under bullets."[46]

Cobb and Brown—whom the general considered a traitor (as well as one of the more unrefined and unscrupulous products of the state's yeoman class)—detested each other, and their feuding only worsened as the war wore on. But the crisis at Macon found the two working in unaccustomed harmony. The governor was in town to help organize and arm his militiamen and send them "on loan" to General John Bell Hood in Atlanta. There almost 2000 of their number were already serving under Brown's hand-picked militia commander, Major General Gustavus Woodson Smith—West Point graduate, former Confederate general, and (briefly) Secretary of War under Jefferson Davis, whom Smith hated bitterly. Obviously, the presence of several thousand militiamen and other troops in Macon complicated Stoneman's plans.[47]

Also available for the coming fight were a variety of Macon's local defense units, including the elderly gentlemen of the "Silver Greys" of the Macon City Battalion and Lieutenant Colonel John W. Mallet's Ordnance Battalion, composed of workers and detailed men assigned to the Confederate armory, arsenal, and laboratory.[48]

After sending one thousand militiamen to defend Milledgeville, Governor Brown turned over the balance of the militia to General Cobb, who took the precaution of sending a regiment east to protect

Brigadier General Robert Toombs, Georgia Militia. Another enemy of the Davis administration—as well as another former Confederate general—the colorful Toombs was chief of General Smith's staff during the Atlanta and Savannah Campaigns. (Hargrett Rare Book and Manuscript Library, University of Georgia Libraries.)

Colonel Thomas Hardeman, Georgia Militia. Another member of Smith's staff, prominent Maconite Hardeman served as adjutant general of the militia division. (Hargrett Rare Book and Manuscript Library, University of Georgia Libraries.)

Lieutenant Colonel John W. Mallet, CSA. A valued ordnance officer, Mallet found himself in command of a local defense unit during Stoneman's Raid. (From Francis T. Miller's *The Photographic History of the Civil War* [1911].)

Griswoldville. As Stoneman neared Macon, Brown attempted to raise more men by distributing a broadside calling to arms the remainder of the able-bodied population. General Cobb—accompanied by an honored guest, General Joseph E. Johnston, recently commander of the Army of Tennessee—took charge of the preparations for battle and sent all available men across the river to East Macon. His force, approximately 2000 strong, was roughly equal to Stoneman's.[49]

On Cobb's left, commanding the direct Macon-Clinton road, a strong Rebel force awaited Adams's Kentuckians. Commanded by Colonel John B. Cumming—commander of Macon's post of Confederate Reserves—this portion of Cobb's force comprised a regiment each of militia and Reserves, plus Mallet's battalion (strengthened by "the Atlanta Wright Guards, a company of seventy-three *refugees*"), all supported by two field pieces.[50]

On the right, facing the bulk of Stoneman's men, two militia regiments under Colonel G. W. Lee occupied the high ground on the George W. Adams farm near Fort Hawkins, where a Confederate battery was emplaced. In reserve near the river was the Macon City Battalion, commanded by Colonel George C. Gibbs, ranking officer at the Confederate post in Macon.[51]

Though the opposing forces were essentially equal in numbers, the Rebel troops were mostly green; few, whether Reserves or militia, had been under hostile fire. But the militia had increasingly attracted criticism from the press and public opinion, especially from those quarters politically opposed to Governor Brown. The Georgia Militia in general, though respected and admired during the Indian wars of the late 1700s and early 1800s, had increasingly become a laughingstock, in part because its diminished effectiveness had provoked published lampoons in the 1830s and 1840s from such Georgia humorists as A. B. Longstreet and William Tappan Thompson. Much more recently, their successor, "Bill Arp" (Charles Henry Smith), had tweaked "Joe Brown's Pets" in several of his newspaper columns.[52]

In antebellum Georgia the gentry and professional classes had generally joined elite volunteer militia companies such as the Macon

# TO THE CITIZENS OF MACON.

## HEAD QUARTERS,
### *Macon, July 30, 1864.*

The enemy is now in sight of your houses. We lack force. I appeal to every man, Citizen or Refugee, who has a gun of any kind, or can get one, to report at the Court House with the least possible delay, that you may be thrown into Companies and aid in the defense of the city. A prompt response is expected from every patriot.

### JOSEPH E. BROWN,

☞ Report to Col. Cary W. Styles, who will forward an organization as rapidly as possible.

This broadside was distributed in the streets of Macon during Stoneman's attack on the city. (Hargrett Rare Book and Manuscript Library, University of Georgia Libraries.)

The southeast blockhouse of Fort Hawkins. In 1864, this structure and another block-house, together with a long barracks building, still stood, though the old frontier fort's stockade walls no longer existed. During Stoneman's attack, an artillery piece was placed in front of the blockhouse and "an officer [was] placed on the tower to spy out [the Federal] positions and direct the shot." A postwar view. (Georgia Department of Archives and History.)

Volunteers, which had been absorbed by Confederate regiments—often en masse—early in the war. The common or standing militia—the target of the antebellum lampoons—was drawn from the yeomanry (or "yokelry," as the humorists had it), now gone from the state in large numbers through volunteering or conscription. At Macon in July 1864, with the organization of the First Division, Georgia Militia, only recently begun, many of the militiamen on the firing line were actually officers (though mostly untried) who had been reduced to the ranks during the crisis. Most had never before seen their newly appointed officers, Confederate convalescents from Macon's hospitals.[53]

## 7.
## GRISWOLDVILLE AND MACON UNDER FIRE

As Cobb's motley force awaited Stoneman on Saturday morning, 30 July, some of Capron's men struck the Central railroad several miles east of Macon. They destroyed track and trains, including stock cars, torched with the animals still aboard. Finding Griswoldville too well defended to enter, the blue troopers rolled burning passenger cars into the village. There the wooden cars were soon "entirely consumed," though, surprisingly, without damage to any nearby structures or to a waiting passenger train. But the flames spread quickly to a line of box cars standing nearby on the siding. The raiders next sent a captured locomotive full-throttle, backwards, into the village. According to a newspaper report, the engine raced into Griswoldville "under a full head of steam and struck the rear car of [the] passenger train, splitting it in two and throwing the two portions on both sides of the track. Continuing, the engine threw off two more cars from the train" before lurching to a stop in the wreckage.[54]

Though Griswoldville itself was saved from destruction, the rolling stock on the siding was all but obliterated. Most of these boxcars belonged to the state-owned Western and Atlantic Railroad—now in the control of the enemy—and were being inhabited by scores of refugees from various points in north Georgia. The burning of these cars left their residents once again homeless, as well as destitute. Among those living in the boxcar village was a Presbyterian divine, the Reverend Doctor John S. Wilson. He and his wife lost all the furniture they had salvaged from their Atlanta home, as well as their winter clothing. Also destroyed were the minister's library and manuscripts, "the labor of forty years," as well as many years' worth of the manuscript minutes of the Synod of Georgia.[55]

In the state's newspapers there was considerable interest in the fate of the Griswoldville pistol works, and some erroneously reported that the factory had been destroyed. But, with the works actually unscathed, Griswold & Gunnison's output would hold steady. Additionally, by the end of August 1864, the firm would gross an additional $4030 by cleaning and repairing almost eight hundred rifles and muskets for the Confederate government.[56]

After their attack on Griswoldville, Capron's men joined Stoneman on the Garrison Road just east of Walnut Creek. Splashing across the shallow stream, the two Yankee brigades scattered Confederate pickets and took the high ground on Captain Sam Dunlap's farm, to the left of the road. There the Federals' two artillery pieces were brought into position in the yard of the farm house, while dismounted cavalrymen, firing their carbines, fanned forward toward Macon's defenders. Though the Yankees' cannonades and volleys created some gaps in the opposing line, it did not break.[57]

Among the militiamen under fire was a sixteen-year-old Clinton boy, Bob Kingman. His company was in line near Fort Hawkins, where the Confederate battery had begun to hammer the Union position. Kingman, armed with an old Mississippi rifle, knelt and fired from among the field's cornstalks, giving a good account of himself.[58]

Not as much could be said for one of his older comrades, "Uncle Mem" Williams. Young Sam Griswold, the pistol-maker's grandson—also

The Confederate Central Laboratory, Macon. One of the few buildings in the Confederacy constructed by the central government, the laboratory was never fully operational and became a barrel factory in later years. No longer extant. (Georgia Department of Archives and History.)

The Macon City Bridge at Fifth Street. This bridge replaced a similar structure washed away in the summer freshet of 1864. (Georgia Department of Archives and History.)

in the militia's ranks that day—remembered that Williams had posed an important question before the battle opened. What should he do, as an old man so crippled with rheumatism that he would not be able to run. "Why we want those who can't run," an officer responded. "You are the very fellow." But, as the Federal fire became heavy, Griswold noticed that Williams's portion of the line ran for the rear, with the rheumatic old man in the lead.[59]

Along with the very young and the very old, convalescents from Macon's hospitals also fought in the East Macon battle. Among them was Campbell Tracy, who had been wounded in Virginia and was still on crutches. He recalled:

> We went into line of battle in a swamp; deployed as skirmishers and were all posted behind trees. I was well flanked: the venerable Dr. [David] Wills, pastor First Presbyterian Church, was on my right; and that good old father in Israel, the Reverend J. E. Evans, Mulberry Street Methodist Church, was on my left, a veteran soldier having thus been *wisely* placed, all along the line between the citizens! Soon Stoneman came up, and the firing commenced. His first advance was repulsed, but he soon got a battery in position, and opened on us with that. A second charge on our line was driven back and everything was going on as lively as in old Virginia when on their third advance a Yank got a side shot at me as I leaned against my tree to shoot. His bullet went between my lip and the bark, the shock knocking me off my crutches. As I fell, the blood flowed freely, my lip having been cut by pieces of the bark.
>
> Old Parsons Wills and Evans quit firing, and ran to my assistance. I told them I was not much hurt; to help me up, and go back and keep firing or the enemy would break through the line! But wishing to help me—*(thinking I needed surgical aid) and knowing they needed to get off the firing line!*—they insisted on picking me up…. They had me hoisted up as high as their shoulders with me just *a kickin' and a cussin'!* Parson Evans said: "Campbell, ain't you afraid to take the name of the Lord in

vain, right here in the presence of death, hell and destruction?" Just then a shell bursted close by. They let me drop and *broke for the rear!* I called to them for God's sake to come back, or the Yanks would break through the line. I *swore some more* and they came back and helped me to my tree. I said to them, as we resumed shooting, "I tell you, boys, you like to have broke my wounded leg over! Don't ever try that stunt again!"[60]

On Cobb's left, Adams's Kentuckians had fought so poorly that their advance was taken for a feint, and most of their opponents marched to strengthen Cobb's right. There the Yankee artillerists had elevated their pieces to fire across the river into Macon. One shell exploded harmlessly outside the Academy Hospital, near the "Bear's Den." Another flew farther and crashed without detonating into the residence of Judge Asa Holt. Both shells were apparently meant to strike the opulent residence of William Butler Johnston, a Confederate treasury official. On a Yankee spy map of Macon, Johnston's Italianate mansion loomed large as a "prominent Secesh" residence visible from a great distance.[61]

Failing to silence the persistent Fort Hawkins battery, and unable to break through the Confederate lines, Stoneman reluctantly decided to fall back. His decision was reinforced by confirmation of the report that the broad city bridge, over which he had meant to cross into Macon, was indeed gone. Undermined by a spring freshet, it had tumbled into the Ocmulgee several weeks before, and its remains still littered the west bank. Attempts to take the floored railroad trestle further downstream had failed because of the resistance of Tracy Campbell and his comrades. Moreover, Stoneman also learned to his chagrin that Camp Oglethorpe was all but empty. At word of his approach, most prisoners had been spirited east by rail. Ironically, their train had cleared Gordon only minutes before the town was struck by Davidson's detachment of the raiders.[62]

So Stoneman, having inflicted some seventy casualties while suffering many fewer himself, left the field to General Cobb, whose guest, General Johnston, took no credit for the victory. Johnston later wrote that he had given Cobb no advice, and that the raiders had been repelled by Cobb's

The "Cannonball House." The house of Judge Asa Holt received this name after being struck by one of Stoneman's shells. The projectile "struck the sand sidewalk, passed through the second column from the left on the gallery, and entered the parlor over a window, landing unexploded in the hall." The wing to the right has now been shifted to the opposite side of the main building; the house and the brick kitchen behind it now serve as a museum. (Georgia Department of Archives and History.)

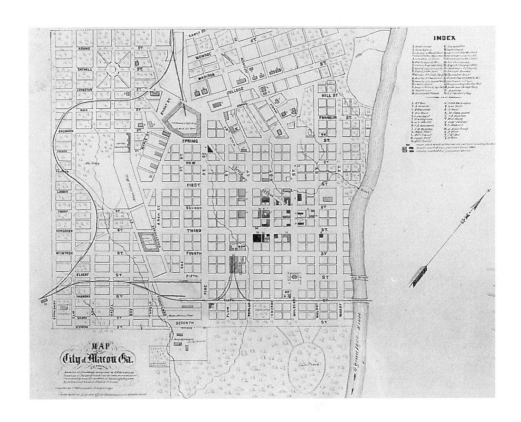

The City of Macon during the Civil War. This Federal map of Macon contained a great deal of information vital to spies or an attacking or occupying force. (National Archives.)

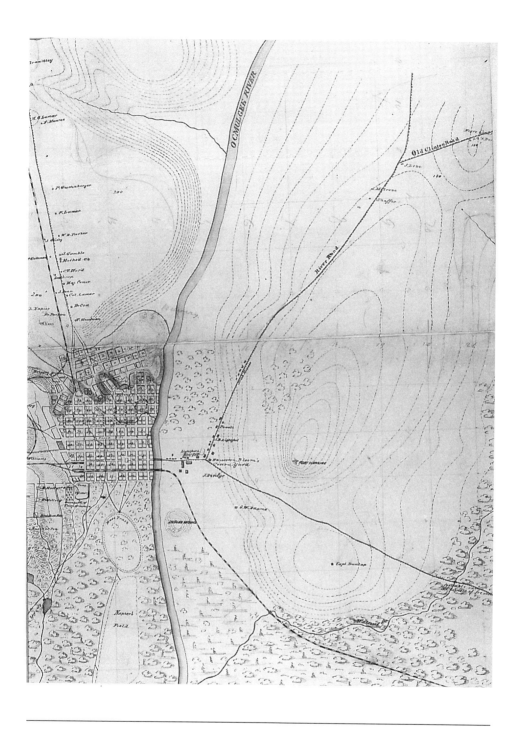

"Map of Macon and Vicinity." This detail of another Federal map of Macon shows the East Macon battlefield. The Confederate forces were at Fort Hawkins and vicinity and up the River Road past the "Irish Houses," facing attacks from the Walnut Creek crossing and the Old Clinton Road, respectively. Stoneman's Rodman guns were posted in the yard of Captain Dunlap's house, on the hill to the lower right. (National Archives.)

Macon from the Female College (Old Wesleyan). This postwar view looks down High
Street toward the river, with East Macon to the left in the haze beyond. The postbellum
courthouse is in the center, with the tall steeple of the First Presbyterian Church (c.
1858) to the right. To the far left, with its soaring chimneys, is Confederate treasury official William Butler Johnston's palatial mansion (c. 1855-1859). Now known as Hay
House, it has been extensively restored and is a popular tourist destination. (From *Art
Work of Macon* [1894].)

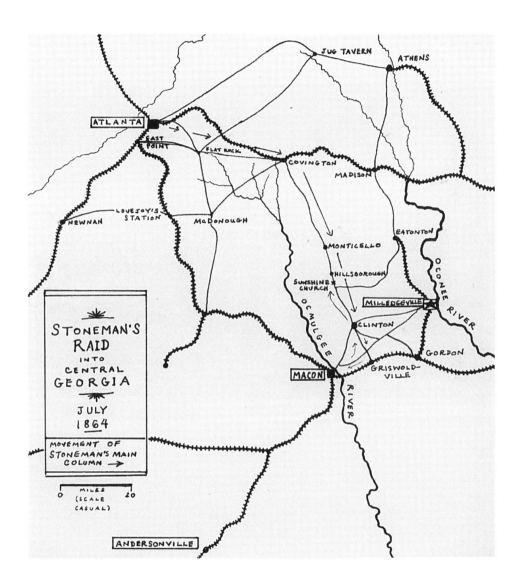

Stoneman's Raid into Central Georgia Courtesy of the author.)

*The Georgia Militia under Gen. Floyd, attacking the Creek Indians at Autossee—Novr 29th, 1813.* This rare engraving (c. 1820) shows the heroic image the Georgia Militia enjoyed during the late 1700s and early 1800s. (Hargrett Rare Book and Manuscript Library, University of Georgia Libraries.)

*Militia—The Parade.* By the 1840s the Georgia Militia had become a source of humor, as seen in this engraving depicting a militia muster at "Pineville," Georgia. (From a post-bellum edition of William Tappan Thompson's *Major Jones's Courtship*, originally published in 1840.)

"own courage and disposition and the excellent conduct of his troops"—including the militiamen, "who heard hostile shot then for the first time."[63]

## 8.
## THE BATTLE OF SUNSHINE CHURCH

Unnerved by the reverses of the day, the exhausted Stoneman found himself torn by indecision. After ordering and canceling several movements, he at last regretfully decided to abandon his major goal of saving the sufferers at Andersonville. Instead, he gave orders for his force to retrace its route at least as far northeast as Hillsboro, where there would be a choice of roads leading back to Sherman's lines.[64]

This decision agitated Stoneman's officers and men. They assumed that dismounted Confederate cavalry had been among their opponents at Macon and would take to the saddle and follow closely on their heels. They also supposed, with far more accuracy, that another force of Rebel horsemen was on their track and descending upon them from the north. In essence, Stoneman's men feared that they were about to be crushed "between the upper and lower millstone."[65]

In fact, a number of Confederate cavalrymen were already astride Stoneman's escape route, solidly barricaded a few miles below Hillsboro. They were part of a 1300-man force—commanded by Clinton-born Brigadier General Alfred Iverson—sent in pursuit of the raiders with orders from Confederate cavalry chieftain Joseph Wheeler to attack the Yankees "wherever found." Iverson's advance had reached Clinton on the afternoon of the Macon battle. Rapidly, his men had rounded up and jailed those raiders who had remained in the vicinity. Then, as dusk approached, Confederate scouts galloped into Clinton, hotly pursued by

Major General Joseph Wheeler, CSA. A native of Augusta, Georgia, Wheeler served as Confederate cavalry commander throughout the Atlanta, Savannah, and Carolinas Campaigns. The final months of the war found him and his troopers attacked in some quarters of the homefront as thieves and vandals. But the McCook-Stoneman Raid presented Wheeler with a dilemma that he met brilliantly. (US Army Military History Institute, Carlisle Barracks, Pennsylvania.)

Brigadier General Alfred Iverson, CSA. Though Clinton-born, Iverson had left his birth-place at an early age. Like Stoneman, he needed to refurbish his reputation in the summer of 1864. He had erred at Gettysburg the previous July and seen his brigade all but destroyed. After the Battle of Sunshine Church, he wrote proudly to his father that the final Confederate charge had scattered the Yankees "like chaff." (Courtesy of Gary Kross, Gettysburg, Pennsylvania.)

the leading horsemen of Stoneman's column. After a brief skirmish in the streets, the Confederates fell back toward their main line below Hillsboro.[66]

Outraged that some of their comrades had been locked up, the raiders emptied the jail and set it afire. Although the exterior walls were stone, the wooden interior blazed up lustily and lighted the way for Stoneman and his men for a distance up the Hillsboro road.[67]

What followed for the Yankees was a hellish night march, contested every mile of the way by Confederate troopers. With alarming frequency, the Federal cavalrymen struck heavy rebel picket lines, often protected by makeshift barricades. As the night wore on, the Union retreat became slower and slower. Finally, after midnight, the exhausted raiders dropped down to rest in the fields of John Barfield's plantation. They had not covered half the distance to Hillsboro.[68]

Mounting up the next morning, Stoneman and his weary men soon passed a tiny log chapel called Sunshine Church. Not far beyond the church, they encountered Iverson's main force. A Confederate battery occupied the center of the Hillsboro road, on a rise that had been fortified with logs and fence rails, barricades that "curved outward like waiting arms." Behind these field works were the Alabama brigade of Brigadier General W. W. Allen (which had been resisting Stoneman's advance), Iverson's own Georgia brigade (under Colonel Charles C. Crews), and the Kentucky brigade of Colonel W. C. P. Breckinridge. "We knew that the enemy had superior numbers," remembered one of the Confederates, "but we trusted to the greater bravery of our troops, and the fact that the enemy would be demoralized by plunder and fatigue."[69]

Stoneman faced a daunting task, for there was no problem "more difficult for a cavalry commander than that of attacking an enemy drawn up for an engagement, unless it [was] withdrawing tired in the face of a fresh and superior foe." Although Stoneman's subordinates argued for breaking out to the right and passing through Eatonton and on to Atlanta, the Yankee general—thwarted too frequently over the past twenty-four hours—was determined to butt his way through the obstructing force.[70]

The birthplace of Brigadier General Alfred Iverson, Clinton. (Courtesy of the Greene-Collins family.)

Brigadier General W. W. Allen, CSA. New York-born, Allen was raised in Alabama. His cavalry brigade, one of the few at full-strength during the Atlanta Campaign, was instrumental in winning the Battle of Sunshine Church. (US Army Military History Institute.)

The terrain was all but impossible for mounted fighting. In the pines to either side of the narrow road the ground fell away sharply into a network of gullies and ravines, pine-shaded and choked with undergrowth. Nonetheless, a demoralizing order came down from Stoneman: Capron's and Adams's men were to charge forward at once on foot. One of the Rodman guns, posted in the center of the road, would provide support. But, understandably, the blue troopers dreaded having to move forward dismounted against a fortified foe, far behind enemy lines. Their feeble advance took them into an enfilading fire and immediately provoked a brisk Confederate countercharge, though the Rebels soon returned to their barricades. The fighting became more sporadic and began to wind down into stalemate.[71]

During a lull in the fighting a rather unattractive young woman appeared within the Yankee lines. Closer inspection revealed her to be a he—a discharged young Jones County soldier named Joe Funderburk, who lived just up the road. He was trying to pass through the enemy lines in one of his mother's dresses. The incident would have been more humorous had it not been for the Yankees' desperate situation—and Stoneman's insistence on branding the boy's escapade as espionage. Funderburk was sent to the rear for future hanging, with orders that he not be allowed to remove his dress.[72]

Colonel Charles C. Crews. CSA. A physician-turned-cavalryman, Crews was one of Wheeler's ablest subordinates. He would end the war disabled by wounds. (Library of Congress.)

Colonel W. C. P. Breckinridge, CSA. A cousin of Major General John C. Breckinridge, he practically destroyed Capron's command at Jug Tavern, several days after Sunshine Church. A postwar image. (From John B. Castleman's *Active Service* [1917].)

# 9.
# THE WAY TO STONEMAN'S HILL

As morning wore into afternoon, the Federals increasingly feared being struck from behind. After more discussion, Stoneman's officers finally persuaded him that the best course would be for his men to break out to the right. The general, however, was determined to remain behind with Colonel Biddle and part of his brigade, to cover the retreat of the others. But, before the brigade commanders could organize their scattered forces for the withdrawal, Confederate shells began to fall among the Yankees with deadly effect. The barrage was soon followed by a noisy charge of the Georgia regiments under Colonel Crews.[73]

Within the raiders' lines, as one of Adams's Kentuckians recalled,

> The shells were flying all about us. I was near Company A, and a shell burst in the midst of it. I heard a groan, and when the smoke and dust cleared away, I saw that Lieutenant Humphrey had his leg shot off. Captain Wolford and some others went to help him, when here came another shell in the same place. After it burst we looked and oh, what a sight. Captain Wolford was lying on the ground, his head nearly torn off by a piece of shell. He was killed so quick that he hardly knew what hurt him. Just then the Rebels charged and we gave way.[74]

The Federals' worst fear suddenly became a reality as a squadron of Rebel horsemen from the Fourth Georgia appeared in the rear, where the raiders' horses were being held. Many of Stoneman's men were cut down as they tried to mount. Those able to get into their saddles struck off at once into the woods. Adding to the confusion, the terrified "Negro Brigade" scattered throughout the area.[75]

As most of the raiders dispersed, Stoneman and his detachment made their stand near the Hillsboro road on a hill that would thereafter bear his name. For the others, retreat soon turned into rout, and rout, in some cases, became a fatal stampede. Panicked horses and their riders tumbled headlong into gullies, then were trampled and mutilated by those who came behind them. The Federals who took Joe Funderburk with them crashed through the undergrowth with such heedless haste that the boy's frock was torn to shreds. When he escaped that night and started home, only the dress's collar remained above his clothes.[76]

Adams's Kentuckians, most rapid and most fortunate in their departure, returned fairly quickly to Sherman's lines with no further losses. Capron's men, on the other hand, wound up on the outskirts of Athens. Repulsed there, they proceeded westward to King's Tanyard, near Jug Tavern. Surprised in their sleep, with their horses unsaddled, Capron's men were badly cut up by a pursuing force of Confederate Kentuckians led by Colonel W. C. P. Breckinridge. Some of the raiders died by drowning when a bridge collapsed as they tried to escape. The survivors—including Capron and his young son—would not limp back into Sherman's lines until well into August.[77]

The maneuvers that concluded the Battle of Sunshine Church had been ordered by Colonel Charles C. Crews, who had been assigned to field command by Iverson. One of Crews's men later recalled the first Confederate charge and the fighting that followed:

> Thirty-eight of our boys were killed and wounded in the charge, among them our first lieutenant. He had his right thigh broken with a Minie ball. He was immediately on my left and came near falling against me. I called Berry Atwood and we carried him off the field and placed him on a stretcher. I went back where I had left my gun and found Lou Reed of Co. E, Carroll County, Georgia lying on his back in the broiling hot sun, with his brains oozing out. A little farther on I found a large Yankee with his thigh broken and two of his comrades lying dead near him. I dragged the poor fellow in the shade of a small pine and I think he died where I left him. As I passed on I found a dead Yankee lying on his face in an old field ditch, shot in the back of the head. The fellow had on Confederate gray pants and Confederate woven suspenders. My suspenders were worn out and I appropriated his and wore them the balance of the war. I then followed the sound of the guns and caught up with the

The Jones County Jail, Clinton, in the late nineteenth century. It survived a burning by Stoneman's Raiders to be dismantled in the early 1900s; its granite blocks were used to build a retaining wall around the new courthouse in Gray. (Georgia Department of Archives and History.)

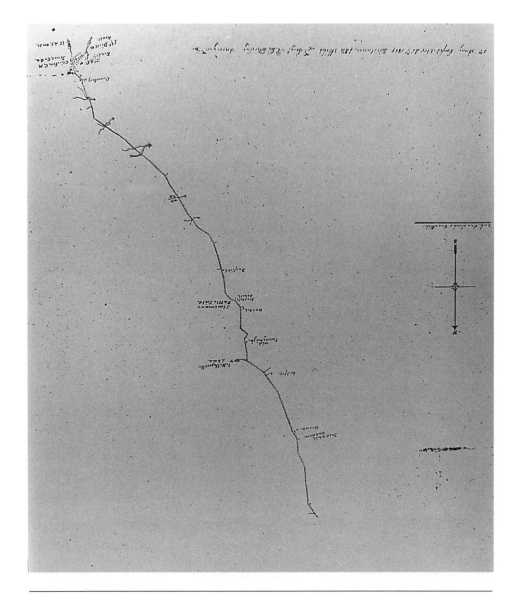

Stoneman's Battlefield, from an unpublished Federal map. Part of a series drafted during the March to the Sea, this map shows the road from Hillsboro to Clinton. Stoneman's men bivouacked on the Barfield plantation (toward the center of the map) the night before the battle at Sunshine Church. The church is marked as "Haskel's School," since it was used for that purpose on weekdays. Many years later, fragments of the students' broken slates still marked the site. The Hascall (proper spelling) house, just north, was used as a field hospital after the battle, as was the church itself. The site of the Funderburk house is also marked, though misspelled. "Stoneman's Battlefield" actually marks Stoneman's Hill, the surrender site; much of the battle was fought to the north, below the Milledgeville road. Joseph C. White's house (no longer extant) was also used as a field hospital—and burial site of some of the dead Federals—and served as Iverson's headquarters. It was here that Stoneman and his officers were brought after the battle. (National Archives.)

balance of my command, about a half mile further on. After several hours fighting, I saw a fellow with a white flag, dressed in blue, come galloping down and I said, "Boys, that's good news."[78]

It *was* good news, especially to old man McKissick. Soon freed from his captors, he returned to a wife certain she was a widow. For Stoneman, of course, the battle's outcome was very bad news indeed—and deeply mortifying—since he now had to surrender himself and the 200-man fragment he commanded. His humiliation, however, was not complete, for he was soon put in the position of having to surrender his sword to a mere colonel. When confronted by Crews, an indignant Stoneman for a time refused to tender his blade, but surrender he finally did. Upon learning that he had been whipped by a force numerically inferior to his own, Stoneman wept—broken by grief, fatigue, and "prostration from blood loss" related to his 1863 ailment.[79]

Along with his sword, Stoneman had lost his two field pieces, approximately 1000 rifles, and scores of horses. Iverson's men, who had suffered fewer than fifty casualties, also rounded up many of the temporarily liberated slaves and sent them back to their masters, with one exception. Minor, a slave of Samuel Griswold who had served as a guide for the raiders, was left hanging from a tree on the battlefield.[80]

Elsewhere on the battlefield, captured Yankees (other than Stoneman's detachment) numbered 300, with almost as many dead and wounded. Some were too badly hurt to be moved immediately, and were cared for at Sunshine Church and nearby at Frank Hascall's house and other residences. Their nurses were ladies of the area, including Clinton's Dr. Palatia Stewart, who held a medical diploma from a Connecticut school. But foremost among those ministering to the men so lately threatening them was Betty Hunt, whose husband was away in Confederate service. Known by the wounded raiders as the "Angel of Sunshine Church," she received a written eulogy from the grateful men whom she had served as nurse, along with a letter to any other Federals who might enter Jones County, asking that they spare the Hunt property. After the war, some of

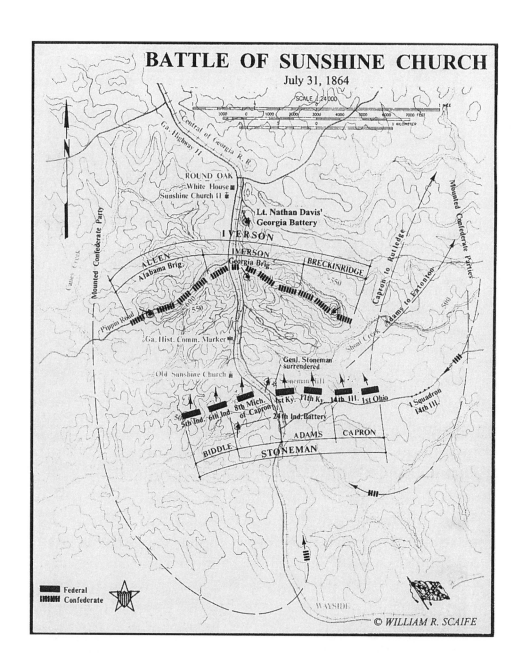

Battle of Sunshine Church (Courtesy of William R. Scaife.)

Betty Hunt, the "Angel of Sunshine Church," who served as one of the nurses of the Federal wounded after Stoneman's defeat. In an affidavit left with her when they were moved, her former patients wrote: "Though she may have suffered pain and hardship, [Mrs. Hunt] has forgotten everything in the natural feelings of a generous and noble disposition, considering only how she could relieve our wants, alleviate our sufferings, visiting us frequently, and soothing our sorrows by friendly words." After the war, some of these men moved to Jones County, and one served among Mrs. Hunt's pallbearers when she died in 1901. By this time another former Yankee soldier had married one of the Hunts' daughters. In this photograph, taken before the war, Mrs. Hunt wears a bracelet woven from her mother's hair. (Courtesy of Mrs. Hunt's granddaughter, Dossie Hunt Teague.)

The Hunt House, near the Sunshine Church battlefield. Built around 1810, this structure, the wartime home of Jesse and Betty Hunt, survives today. During the March to the Sea, there was extensive vandalism and slaughter of stock at the Hunt plantation, as well as confiscation or destruction of over $5000 worth of property, including jewelry, silverware, ten bales of cotton, and two thousand pounds of meat. Several of Stoneman's former raiders worked well into the early 1900s in an unsuccessful attempt to have the Federal government reimburse the Hunts. (Georgia Department of Archives and History.)

Sunshine Church II. Built in 1880, this structure replaced the first church, which was burned during Sherman's March. In 1889 B. F. Morris—a former raider who had been wounded and disabled at the Battle of Sunshine Church—was invited south and preached at the new chapel. Later, Jesse Hunt accepted an invitation to address the August 1890 reunion of the Sherman Brigade in Ohio. Upon rising to speak, he examined a piece of silverware and, on replacing it, said, "Just checking to see if it was mine." After the laughter died, Hunt delivered a New South oration and, afterwards, the veterans "pressed upon him from all sides eager to grasp him by the hand." (Georgia Department of Archives and History.)

Stoneman's Raiders moved to Jones County, where they attempted to get restitution for damages to the Hunt plantation, and ultimately served among Mrs. Hunt's pallbearers.[81]

After the Battle of Sunshine Church, reported one of the Confederates, "General Iverson and staff went back to the house of Mr. Joseph White, and there received General Stoneman and his officers, giving them their parole for the time[;] they were allowed perfect liberty till delivered over to the authorities." This was much better treatment than a Confederate newspaper demanded: a "cell and a shaved head" for Stoneman.[82]

Almost 500 Yankee prisoners were finally escorted to Macon. There the "dejected and haggard" Stoneman and several of his officers were enclosed in the Camp Oglethorpe stockade they had come to empty. And some of his raiders were soon shut up in box cars for what would be, for some of them, a one-way trip to Andersonville.[83]

Iverson's cavalry was given a warm welcome by the relieved and jubilant Maconites. To go with the grateful words, the Rebel troopers also received a purse of $700 from the ladies of Macon. The men spent it every bit on watermelons, and followed their feast with a boisterous battle of melon rinds.[84]

## 10.
## CONFEDERATE THANKSGIVING

The rejoicing proved short-lived. Despite repeated calls in the press for his execution, Stoneman was soon exchanged to raid again—though back in Virginia this time, far from the scene of his latest failure. It would not be Stoneman, but Major General William T. Sherman, who would soon become the focus of middle Georgians' fears. In early September, Sherman

Major General William T. Sherman, USA. According to Sherman, "War's legitimate object is a more perfect peace," but his actions against the civilian population in Georgia in 1864 reverberate to this day. (Georgia Department of Archives and History.)

Major General O. O. Howard, USA. A pious West Pointer who had lost an arm at Seven Pines, Howard had been one of G. W. Smith's students at West Point during his senior year. He personally stood by to send reinforcements during the critical stages of the affair at Griswoldville, and relished the fact that it was Smith who had taught him "how to recognize and take 'a military position.'" (Massachusetts Commandery, Military Order of the Loyal Legion, and the US Army Military History Institute.)

finally flanked Hood from Atlanta, and he and his army were soon comfortably ensconced within the city's fortifications. Despite some military excursions, the Yankees still occupied the city in early November, as Confederate Thanksgiving approached. By that time, the citizenry south of Atlanta found their thankfulness mixed uncomfortably with dread. But in Griswoldville, Messrs. Griswold and Gunnison—having failed to rent the pistol works to some other entrepreneurs as they had wished—continued to turn out revolvers with commendable efficiency.[85]

Despite growing fears below Atlanta, the underlying reason for the Thanksgiving celebration—the fall harvest—remained. In 1864 that harvest was abundant (despite the fact that Confederate impressment and the tax-in-kind would take much of it). The slaves gathered food and forage crops, as did the militiamen. After Atlanta's fall these troops had been placed by Governor Brown on "agricultural leave," in part to prevent their being gathered into the Confederate army. In all, Brown had finally been able to arm and field over 10,000 of his citizen-soldiers during the Atlanta Campaign.[86]

By 16 November, when Thanksgiving services were being held in Georgia's churches, Hood had left the state to move against Sherman's supply base in Tennessee. With Sherman's future movements the subject of anxious speculation, the Thanksgiving services probably included as many supplications as thanks. But in Macon's Christ Church, the liturgy for the day did include a prayer of gratitude for "deliverance from enemies." This would prove decidedly premature, for the previous day—15 November, 1864—Sherman's "Grand Army" had begun marching south, destination unknown. The Thanksgiving season, itself fraught with fears, would soon be recognized as only a foretaste of a grimmer harvest to come.[87]

# 11.
# MARCHING TOWARD THE SEA

As another harbinger, the Federal army's last night in Atlanta proved most unpeaceful. Flames meant to consume railway facilities found hidden Confederate munitions as well. Thunderous explosions threw heavy showers of debris into parts of the city. Some smoldering fragments disturbed Sherman's slumbers by striking dangerously near his quarters in Judge Richard F. Lyon's house. Throughout the night the inferno raged, a portent of future fires.[88]

The night's "hideous turmoil" gave place the next morning to the sounds of drums, martial music, and songs, as the huge army of over 60,000 men—a number almost three times greater than the population of Savannah, Georgia's largest city—prepared to abandon the ruins of Atlanta. Sherman's next goal lay seaward, for he was bent on capturing Savannah and devastating the heartland that stretched before it.[89]

With Hood's army striking into Tennessee, Confederate resistance to Sherman's undertaking would have to be minimal. Hood's thrust had left Georgia dangerously open to an invading army, for no other appreciable force could be sent to protect the state. Only a small and very mixed force remained to contest the Federal advance: 3500 of Wheeler's cavalrymen; some 3000 available militia and other state troops, under Major General Gustavus Woodson Smith; General Cobb's meager force of Confederate Reserves (along with a sprinkling of Confederate army units); and a handful of assorted ad hoc local defense troops.[90]

These troops could not present a formidable threat to Sherman's operations. Wheeler's desertion-plagued command—worn ragged by long months of campaigning—was ill-equipped, poorly fed, and badly mounted. Increasingly, the butternut troopers were feared and despised by many Georgians. Some citizens, in fact, considered Wheeler's men worse than the Federal cavalry in seizing horses and in plundering generally.[91]

Smith's state troops also suffered from desertions and a poor public image. The militiamen—particularly the officers—had long been ridiculed as "Joe Brown's Pets," for the Georgia Militia reputedly provid-

Brigadier General Judson Kilpatrick, USA. Aggressive—but also erratic and careless—
Kilpatrick compiled a mixed record during the March to the Sea. Sherman chose him
as his cavalry commander because of his audacity, but, according to one critic,
Kilpatrick lacked both "integrity" and "a fundamental sense of human decency."
(Massachusetts Commandery, Military Order of the Loyal Legion, and the US Army
Military History Institute.)

A relic of Kilpatrick's cavalry. This saber was found near Cork, west of the Ocmulgee River. (Courtesy of William G. Moffat III.)

ed a haven where officers' commissions and other exemptions protected the governor's political cronies, as well as other conscription-age men who were dodging the enrolling officers. During the summer campaign, after some had made their combat debut at Macon, the "Pets" had largely been confined to the entrenchments protecting Atlanta. Though some had seen combat there (and been praised for their gallantry by General Hood), the militia had generally experienced relatively little of the battlefield. Additionally, huge numbers of them had not responded when summoned back to service after their recent leave. Only the men of the Georgia State Line—a tiny portion of the state troops recently put under Smith's command—closely resembled Confederate infantry in age and experience. They should have, since they represented Governor Brown's only success in creating a conscription-age state "army."[92]

Though the numbers of Cobb's Reserves were small enough, even fewer were available for field service—many were already serving garrison duty at such points as Andersonville, Augusta, and Savannah. And Georgia's ad hoc local defense forces, despite a willingness to serve, were the most inexperienced and widely scattered of the lot.[93]

While Sherman confidently assumed the weakness of any force that might oppose his march, he chose not to depend entirely on his enemy's powerlessness. Though arguably a better general than George B. McClellan, Sherman shared McClellan's distaste for committing his men to battle. To reduce the chances of any Confederate troops being gathered to obstruct him, Sherman split his force into two wings that could simultaneously threaten Augusta and Macon, the two major remaining cities of Georgia's "great munitions complex." Sherman accompanied the left wing, composed of the Fourteenth and Twentieth Corps, Major General Henry W. Slocum commanding. It moved southeast, ostensibly against Augusta, site of the Confederacy's vast powder mill. The right wing, commanded by one-armed Major General Oliver O. Howard, comprised the Fifteenth and Seventeenth Corps and was initially accompanied by 5000 cavalrymen under Brigadier General Judson Kilpatrick. Howard and Kilpatrick were to move south and demonstrate against Macon, an obvious target because of its ordnance facilities. Sherman intended for the available Confederate forces to concentrate at Macon and Augusta, leaving unprotected his immediate goal: Milledgeville, Georgia's capital. Below Milledgeville, the two wings were to draw more closely together to complete their push to Savannah and the sea.[94]

Having abandoned their lines of communication and supply, the two wings marched down separate sets of roads, leaving Atlanta's "pall of smoke" for the bracing autumn air of the countryside. Between the front and rear guards of the columns, the roadways were filled with infantrymen and considerable wheeled traffic: wagons of ammunition and supplies, pontoon trains, artillery, and ambulances. Adding to the noise and commotion of Howard's columns was a large herd of beef cattle. Along the roadsides, train guards marched as best they could, alert to threats from Wheeler's horsemen. Other soldiers were assigned the more diverting task of foraging "liberally" from the land and its inhabitants.[95]

Unlike the last Union cavalry commander to strike into central Georgia, Judson Kilpatrick could not be accused of a lack of nerve. To the contrary, his dash and his penchant for risking both man and mount had won him the nickname "Kil-Cavalry." Various brother officers had argued against Sherman's choice to lead his horsemen, but he ignored them. He agreed that Kilpatrick was "a hell of a damned fool" but noted that this was just the sort of man he wanted to lead his cavalry during the campaign for Savannah. Kilpatrick's activities would be extremely important, for—if the enemy was to be deceived about Sherman's intentions—the Federal cavalry would need to be very effective in screening the infantry's movements with confounding feints and audacious raids.[96]

## 12.
# RESISTING THE MARCH

Leaving Atlanta in advance of Howard's columns, Kilpatrick's cavalry immediately began skirmishing with Wheeler's troopers, from Lovejoy's Station (where they scattered the Confederate cavalry and recaptured Stoneman's Rodman guns) to Bear Creek Station and southeast to the Towaliga River. From the first it seemed that the Rebel horsemen would prove more annoying than dangerous. General Smith's militiamen—who were also in Kilpatrick's path—did not even provide annoyance. They marched quickly from Lovejoy's Station to Griffin, then on to Forsyth. There they greeted with shouts of joy the train that would carry them to the fortifications of Macon.[97]

In Macon, the time had come for desperate measures, and pleas for reinforcements continuously hummed over the telegraph wires. General Cobb, while warning of the "formidable" movement against Macon, also took the practical step of sending to safety several loads of the city's supplies, as well as much of the invaluable armament machinery. Robert Toombs telegraphed Governor Brown that only an infusion of troops could keep Macon from being evacuated entirely. And from Milledgeville, Governor Brown wired his inveterate opponent President Davis to implore him to send the needed regiments. Brown also requested—and was granted by the General Assembly—a *levy en masse*: every white man in Georgia able to bear arms was ordered to the front. Ultimately, few Georgians responded to the levy, and very few Confederate reinforcements arrived.[98]

The word from Virginia was that there were few troops to spare; in place of adequate reinforcements came advice. President Davis suggested that slaves fell trees to block some roads, and that other thoroughfares be planted with pressure-sensitive explosives. General Robert E. Lee counseled that Wheeler's cavalry could "do much." Georgia's Confederate congressmen exhorted their constituents to rise up as one to "assail the invader."[99]

These words had no calming effect in Macon. By 17 November, the city was in a frenzy of activity and fear. Numerous shops closed their doors, and a stream of citizens began crowding onto trains that would take them to the southern and western areas of the state. Then reports came that the Yankee columns had veered away from Macon, toward Jackson. Southeastward at Cork, Kilpatrick's men reassembled. Having dispersed Wheeler's troopers and pillaged extensively, the Federal cavalry crossed the Ocmulgee. At Indian Springs and northward, the elements of the right wing began to converge, bound for the river at Seven Islands, the location of several water-powered factories and mills. There a Federal detachment seized the ferry flat, crossed to the east bank, and took up a defensive position. From the west bank, Union engineers strung two pontoon bridges across the muddy waters, as blue regiments began to clog the roads leading to the bridgeheads.[100]

On 18 November Howard's wing began its crossing: every man, horse, cow, wagon, and field piece had to be channeled across the swaying bridges and up the rain-slickened slopes on the opposite bank. The movement did not stop with nightfall, for huge bonfires illuminated the crossing, as did the flames consuming nearby Planters' Factory.[101]

An army divided at a river crossing is an army at risk, so it was with some alarm that the first regiments to cross came to a halt to listen to heavy firing to their rear. Wheeler's men, it transpired, were not involved. Instead, the gunshots marked the destruction of numerous broken down cattle and horses that were unable to continue the march.[102]

After passing over the river, the right wing's two corps separated. They would not reunite until they reached Gordon, forty miles distant, where they would temporarily park their wagons. The Seventeenth Corps proceeded along an easterly route through Monticello, toward Hillsboro and Blountsville, while the Fifteenth Corps marched nearer to Macon, heading toward concentration at Clinton.[103]

These marching plans were clear enough, but a dreaded development complicated them. Rain—cold and constant—settled heavily over Middle Georgia and impeded the wagon train's progress up the steep hills beyond the Ocmulgee. As the downpours persisted, the roads became all but

THE PARRISH HOUSE

The Parrish House, Kilpatrick's headquarters when Clinton was first occupied. (Engraving from Richard Henry Hutchings, *Hutchings, Bonner, Wyatt: An Intimate Family History* [1937]. Courtesy of the Genealogy Room, Washington Memorial Library, Macon, Georgia.)

Major General Peter J. Osterhaus, USA. A Prussian native with a heavy accent, Osterhaus distinguished himself on many battlefields and was particularly praised for his service during the Vicksburg and Chattanooga Campaigns. (Massachusetts Commandery, Military Order of the Loyal Legion, and the US Army Military History Institute.)

impassable, and the slowed and bogged wagons made tempting targets for roaming squadrons of Confederate cavalry. Concerned by this predicament, the Prussian commander of the Fifteenth Corps, Major General Peter Osterhaus, left behind at the river one entire division, to guard the rear of the train. Osterhaus's remaining three divisions then began plodding over muddy roads toward Clinton, across sodden fields and through dripping patches of pine trees.[104]

## 13.
## CLINTON OCCUPIED

Well in advance of the infantry and the wagons, the lead elements of Kilpatrick's cavalry rode into Clinton after dark on 19 November. Finding the town all but abandoned, the blue horsemen captured six Confederate troopers and a cache of supplies, including horse feed conveniently sacked for hauling.[105]

Clinton's location made it an ideal springboard for raids, since roads intersecting there radiated toward Milledgeville, Gordon, Griswoldville, Irwinton, and Macon. Consequently, Kilpatrick ordered his men to camp in the vicinity, while he himself set up headquarters in the Richard Hutchings house, a stone's throw from the road down which the Fifteenth Corps would soon pass. Soon infantry regiments arrived and encamped south of the town.[106]

One Union infantry officer looked at Clinton with an eye toward more than strategy. Captain George W. Pepper of the Eightieth Ohio was charmed by the town and its surroundings: "The situation of Clinton is that of calm, quiet, peaceful solitude, embowered by trees, which add by their shade a degree of beauty and repose to the scene. The country round it presents a very fine aspect, being well cultivated and ornamented. A little hill, standing to the westward of the town [Bonner's Hill], commands a view of a rich and cultivated valley."[107]

After several days of enemy occupation, Clinton presented a much different appearance to another Ohio officer. He found it to be "a muddy, dirty, dilapidated Southern town," and well he might, for Clinton suffered much during the stay of the Federal forces. Some destruction could be blamed on the cold weather, since many fences and dismantled outbuildings quickly disappeared into campfires. But many other acts came under the heading of Sherman's intent to "make Georgia howl." These included vandalism of the courthouse and some of its records and the razing of the school house and Morgan's Tannery, along with the burning of a number of residences and other structures.[108]

One Clinton resident described the condition of the town after the invaders had departed: "Many of us are utterly ruined—hundreds of our people are without anything to eat—their stock of cattle, hogs, are killed, horses and mules with wagons taken off—all through our streets and commons are to be seen dead horses and mules—entrails of hogs and cattle killed, and in many instances, the hams only taken—oxen and carts even taken away so that we are not able to remove this offensive matter." At the edge of town, Bonner's Hill, which had presented such a fine panorama to Captain Pepper, now lacked a structure at its summit: Richard Bonner's house, the former Griswold residence, was in ashes, along with one-third of the structures in Clinton.[109]

Clinton's environs were also plundered and devastated, and livestock theft in particular brought fatal consequences in one case. During her hurried attempts to hide family belongings from the pillaging soldiers, Mrs. Giles Griswold accidentally ignited a store of gunpowder and was horribly burned. On her isolated plantation, no horse or mule remained for anyone to ride for timely medical help. After lingering painfully, she died on 12 December 1864.[110]

In an open letter in the *Macon Telegraph*, two Clintonians warned those "Refugees of Jones County" (who had fled their homes before the enemy's arrival) that they should expect devastation upon their return: "The whole country around is a wide waste of destruction. Corn cribs, gin

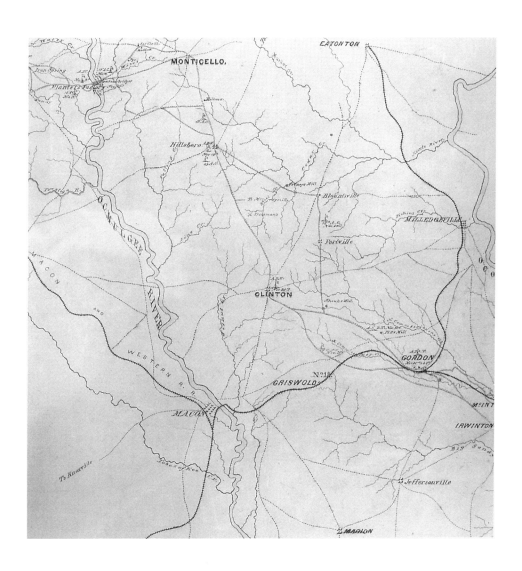

The Central Georgia Area of Operations during the March to the Sea, showing the march routes of the 15th and 17th Corps. From a Federal map. (National Archives.)

Lieutenant General William J. Hardee, CSA. A native of the Georgia coast, Hardee was tasked with defending his home state—with a pitifully small army—against Sherman's four strong corps. (From Francis T. Miller's *The Photographic History of the Civil War* [1911].)

houses, mills, barns, and many residences are all for the most part gone.... Nearly all of the bacon, corn, fodder, wheat, flour, syrup &c., was taken or destroyed." The writers stressed, however, that in this desolate land one thing remained: "an undying hatred towards the Yankees and eternal resistance to their tyrannical sway."[111]

But, in a sense, Clinton had been fortunate. A nearby county seat, Irwinton, lost all its "principal buildings" to the flames. Hillsboro, a Federal officer noted, "<u>was</u> an insignificant town but is in ashes now." So was nearby Sunshine Church, as if its destruction would obliterate the memory of what another Union officer described as the "disgraceful affair" that had occurred there.[112]

When Sherman's right wing entered central Georgia, there had been no illusion that the Confederate authorities could prevent such widespread destruction. Indeed, it was questionable whether they could defend and protect the area's most significant military prize, Macon. When Wheeler and most of his command reached that city about midnight on 19 November, they found Smith's militiamen already in the city, manning some of its northern fortifications. Wheeler also discovered that he had a new superior, Lieutenant General William J. Hardee, who had been given command of all Confederate forces (such as they were) south of the Chattahoochee River. Hardee himself had reached Macon several hours earlier and—informed of the Federal cavalry's arrival in Clinton—ordered Wheeler to move there the next morning to learn what he could of the enemy's strength, position, and intentions.[113]

Setting out before dawn on 20 November, Wheeler advanced toward Clinton with most of his force, while Colonel Charles C. Crews was left behind with his brigade to guard the Garrison Road into East Macon. Wheeler and his men were delayed at first by small detachments of Kilpatrick's cavalry and then found themselves slowed by thick fog as they neared the courthouse town. So dense was the fog that the Confederate general and his escort almost blundered into the advance column of the Fifteenth Corps, which was just arriving in town. Under the fog's cover, six Rebel horsemen captured General Osterhaus's orderly within twenty feet of Yankee headquarters. But, despite this daring thrust, Wheeler failed in his most important objective. He took Hardee little information regarding the enemy's numbers and plans.[114]

Leaving behind detachments to harass the gathering Union forces, Wheeler sent other troopers to picket various strategic roads. Then, riding back toward Macon, he encountered a courier who brought alarming news: Colonel Crews had been ordered to leave his position and ride east to protect the Central railroad from a wrecking crew of Yankee cavalry. This abandonment of the Garrison Road position, Wheeler knew, left East Macon open to a surprise attack. Hurrying to the vulnerable point, the young general found his worst fears confirmed.[115]

By the time Wheeler arrived, several Federal cavalry regiments, supported by artillery, had rushed past the fortified Walnut Creek bridge and advanced a mile farther, where they had captured a redoubt blocking the road. But the arrival of Wheeler, as well as reinforcements from Macon, prevented the blue troopers from doing as much damage as they wished. Some 1100 Confederate troops, commanded by Colonel Stephen H. Colmes of the 50th Tennessee Regiment, were finally brought against Kilpatrick. Colmes's force comprised mainly convalescents (two regiments), as well as batterymen serving as infantry and some volunteer companies, including one from the Blind School Hospital.[116]

Unlike Stoneman's men, Kilpatrick's troopers were prevented from lobbing shells into Macon or destroying the railroad trestle at the creek. Instead, they soon retired eastward toward Griswoldville, tearing up track as they went. The *Macon Telegraph* listed only two Confederates wounded and one killed in the skirmish, while the Federals had lost a dozen horses. The newspaper also reported that "a Yankee had run off and left his foot and leg in a boot down on the bank of Walnut Creek."[117]

The man who destroyed Griswoldville. Captain Frederick S. Ladd of the 9th Michigan Cavalry, with "one hundred picked men," burned the pistol factory and many other structures in Griswoldville on 20 November 1864. Ladd had little over two weeks to live. On 7 December he was killed in action near Savannah at Cypress Swamp. (Burton Historical Collection, Detroit Public Library, Detroit, Michigan.)

Lieutenant Lavender R. Ray, CSA. Iverson's ordnance officer, Ray kept a record of his impressions of Sherman's March, including brief but vivid descriptions of Macon and Griswoldville. (From *Letters and Diary of Lieut. Lavender R. Ray, 1861-1865*, compiled and edited by his daughter, Ruby Felder Ray Thomas.)

# 14.
# GRISWOLDVILLE DESTROYED

Like Macon, Samuel Griswold's industrial village had also been targeted for a raid on 20 November. That morning Captain Frederick S. Ladd had struck out for Griswoldville with "100 picked men of the Ninth Michigan Volunteer Cavalry." Kilpatrick's orders had specified that these troopers were to destroy all railway facilities at the village, as well as all public buildings. Initially alarmed by the sight of Wheeler's pickets, the raiders detoured into the woods to avoid them. Meanwhile, a train steamed through, carrying Governor Brown from Milledgeville to Macon.[118]

Then, shortly after 10:00 A.M., the Yankees charged into Griswoldville, shattering the Sunday stillness. Driving out the few defenders and "keeping them at bay," Ladd and his men began torching the smaller factories and the mills and broke open the major prize, the gun works. Completed pistols were seized and the machinery wrecked before the building was set aflame.[119]

The railroad depot was also destined for burning, but not before a few of the Yankee cavalrymen had some fun. One of them had been a telegrapher in civilian life and succeeded in reaching the Macon telegraph operator from the depot. The Federal wag asked the Rebel operator to convey the compliments of Generals Kilpatrick and Howard to Macon's Confederate commander, and promised that the generals would be visiting in Macon the following day. Undaunted, the Macon telegrapher replied that the Confederate forces in Macon would warmly welcome Kilpatrick and Howard and would even hospitably offer them the quarters recently vacated by General Stoneman.[120]

Some rolling stock of the Western and Atlantic railroad stood on the siding at Griswoldville, and a dozen of the box cars—some containing locomotive parts—were burned, and a locomotive was wrecked. After destroying a lengthy section of track, the raiders were struck by Crews's cavalry brigade. The Yankees then forced a hostage to show them a safe route out of the village, which was soon re-entered by Wheeler's men.

Ladd's men had destroyed the heart of Griswoldville at the cost of three men captured and one "wounded slightly in the hip." Shortly after Crews and his men occupied the village, other units of Kilpatrick's cavalry arrived and again pushed the Rebel horsemen out. The evening of 20 November found the blue troopers camping for the night in and around Griswoldville.[121]

In Macon on the afternoon of 20 November, battle noises drifted from across the river and straggling Rebel cavalry appeared in the streets. The night brought only uneasiness, for, though the Federal attack on East Macon had been repelled with little loss or damage, the threat remained of another attack—perhaps a night assault. In fact, anything was possible. The broken telegraph line and Wheeler's failure to bring back adequate information left General Hardee almost entirely ignorant regarding the situation developing east of the city. The lack of telegraphic communication was particularly troubling, for it left Macon isolated from Savannah and Richmond. Hardee and his fellow officers pondered their dilemma during the wintry night while, in the cold trenches north and east of the town, Macon's defenders kept vigil.[122]

No further cavalry attacks were made on Macon. But the morning of 21 November found Kilpatrick's men very active elsewhere. While some detachments picketed the Garrison Road to discourage Rebel sorties from Macon, others ranged widely, foraging and plundering. Still more busied themselves destroying the rail line in the vicinity of Griswoldville, and the village itself received more thorough damage than the previous day; several buildings and homes that had escaped the torch on Sunday were burned. The Griswold mansion, in fact, was one of the few structures spared—since it was serving as Kilpatrick's new headquarters. Even the slave quarters were reduced to ashes. While some blue troopers repulsed halfhearted attacks from squads of Rebel cavalry, others tore up track. A few spent the day in more leisurely fashion. They were spotted sitting near the ruins in salvaged parlor chairs, roasting potatoes in the hot ashes of burned houses.[123]

Although General Howard would have preferred that Kilpatrick capture and hold East Macon—or at least continue to press it—he had

*Marching in the Rain*. Two etchings by Edwin Forbes, one showing a pontoon wagon stuck in the mud. Though based on operations in another theater of war, Forbes's images often evoke the terrain and the scenes of the March to the Sea (Courtesy of the Dover Pictorial Archives Series.)

*Hauling Artillery*. This etching by Edwin Forbes depicts a situation very similar to that faced by the Federals on the road to Mountain Springs. (Courtesy of the Dover Pictorial Archives Series.)

reluctantly approved the cavalry commander's change of location to Griswoldville. Howard had more pressing problems. By 21 November he had received the good news that Georgia's capital, Milledgeville, had been captured by the advance of the Union left wing. But there was bad news as well, for a potentially disastrous situation had begun to develop for Howard's right wing, still moving through Jones County. The roads between the Ocmulgee and the village of Gordon—Howard's immediate goal—had been lashed by seemingly endless downpours. Overburdened by the stream of infantry columns, wagons, and cattle, the drenched roads had been "torn and churned" into muddy sloughs. Hauling Kilpatrick's artillery over such roads from the Ocmulgee to Clinton killed ten horses, and a piercingly cold wind warned of worse weather to come. By the next day the pontoon trains would bog and freeze in place. For now, the progress of the trains slowed almost to a standstill, as Howard's pioneers began the burdensome work of corduroying the roads with logs.[124]

Meanwhile, Wheeler's cavalry became increasingly bold and persistent. This growing audacity worried Howard, whose wagons were having difficulty staying together and in motion. In his mind the Union general conjured up a horrible picture of his "long, snaky trains" of supplies and munitions "cut asunder" and destroyed piecemeal. As Howard well knew, Wheeler had accomplished just such a destructive feat the previous year in Tennessee's Sequatchie Valley.[125]

# 15.
# GENERAL HOWARD'S STRATAGEM

After the Seventeenth Corps had reached safety in Gordon on the afternoon of the 21 November, General Howard decided to divide Osterhaus's Fifteenth Corps in an effort to protect the threatened wagon train. He ordered two of Osterhaus's divisions—those of Brigadier Generals Charles R. Woods and William B. Hazen—to march from Clinton to Irwinton (several miles southeast of Gordon) on a road passing three miles east of Griswoldville. Accompanied only by the vital ordnance wagons, and thus traveling light, they would provide a protective barrier for the supply train, which—accompanied by Brigadier General John E. Smith's division—would move down the more easterly "direct road" to Gordon. Hazen would leave behind in Clinton one of his brigades, under orders to fortify the town. The brigade would then wait for the last of the wagons to arrive from the Ocmulgee and escort the train to safety.[126]

As an added precaution, Howard ordered the divisions of the protective column to spend the night of 21 November near Griswoldville, camped within supporting distance of each other. Hazen's division would bivouac just north of the Garrison Road near a rural church, Pitts Chapel; Woods's division would camp at the crossroads east of Griswoldville. The next morning, one of Woods's brigades was to make a demonstration toward Griswoldville. Howard hoped that this would discourage a possible enemy sortie from Macon where—Howard had been erroneously informed—15,000 Confederate troops had gathered. At the least, Howard's troops' activities would perhaps divert Wheeler's attention from the creeping wagon train.[127]

Also on the afternoon of 21 November, General Hardee was seeking a way out of a possibly catastrophic predicament of his own. Since no further attack had been made on Macon, Hardee had been proven correct in his assumption that the previous day's assault had been a feint. But if Macon was indeed safe, it was Hardee's duty to move the state troops—over whom he had been given control—to the more vulnerable points in

Lieutenant General Richard Taylor, CSA. Taylor persuaded General Cobb that Macon was safe from Sherman, but he urged that the state troops should be "called back at once." He also witnessed Cobb's discomfort at playing host to Governor Brown, just escaped from Milledgeville, but recorded that Cobb ultimately "yielded to the ancient jest, that for the time being we had best hang together, as there seemed a possibility of enjoying that amusement separately."(Hargrett Rare Book and Manuscript Library, University of Georgia Libraries.)

Georgia. Consequently, he decided (as Sherman intended that he would) that Augusta, with its powder mill, was most in need of protection. Still unaware of what was happening to the east, Hardee assumed that Sherman's right wing had gone from Clinton to Milledgeville. He therefore determined to send the state troops along the line of the Central railroad past the broken track to rail transportation. Having sent a courier south to wire Savannah for a troop train, Hardee calculated that the state soldiers could probably board the cars as nearby as Gordon, twenty miles and a full day's march away. They would then be some 140 rail miles (perhaps only eight hours) from Augusta. To begin the troop movement, Hardee ordered Brigadier General Reuben W. Carswell's First Brigade of the Georgia Militia to leave Macon that afternoon. The remaining three militia brigades were to follow the next morning, accompanied by other state troops and a Confederate battery. Unknown to Hardee, much of the line between Macon and Gordon was already aswarm with enemy cavalrymen, and Gordon itself, captured that morning, was steadily filling with Federal foot soldiers.[128]

In part Hardee could blame Wheeler and his men for this ill-conceived plan. But the Confederate troopers had their best day of fighting on 21 November—despite a morning setback on the Garrison Road near Macon, where a unit was dispersed by Yankee sabers. Later, Confederate Colonel W. C. P. Breckinridge and his Kentucky brigade hit a Federal cavalry regiment below Clinton and drove them for over a mile. Then, during the early afternoon, Rebel horsemen began to push against Kilpatrick at Griswoldville, trying to dislodge the Yankees from the rail line. Reporting these assaults to General Howard, Kilpatrick assured him that his cavalry was "firmly settled and fastened upon the railroad" and could repulse any attack made by Wheeler. Nonetheless, Kilpatrick and his men were soon pushed east from Griswoldville, thus opening the road north to Clinton. Galloping up this road, a detachment of Wheeler's men surprised the train guards of Woods's division, who were bound with their wagons toward encampment at the crossroads. Though the Rebel troopers inflicted some damage, determined resistance soon forced them to withdraw, and the

Brigadier General Charles C. Walcutt, USA. An Ohioan who had been wounded at Shiloh, Walcutt took another wound at Griswoldville. (Massachusetts Commandery, Military Order of the Loyal Legion, and the US Army Military History Institute.)

Colonel Robert F. Catterson, USA. Son of an Irish immigrant, Catterson was not quite thirty when he took field command at Griswoldville after Walcutt fell. Reconstruction found him in Arkansas, commanding black militiamen against the Ku Klux Klan. (Massachusetts Commandery, Military Order of the Loyal Legion, and the US Army Military History Institute.)

Federals constructed barricades to discourage more attacks from that quarter.[129]

That night General Hardee left Macon for Savannah. Going south by rail to Albany, he then rode cross-country to Thomasville to take the train northeast to the coast. Meanwhile, Wheeler's cavalry had camped in and around Griswoldville. There General Wheeler—like Kilpatrick—had set up headquarters in the Griswold residence, which had barely been saved from Yankee torches by house servants. That evening the Rebel horsemen continued their sporadic attacks against the nearby Yankee forces. Three of the blue cavalry regiments had pitched their tents two miles east of the ruined village, with Little Sandy Creek to their front (lightly picketed), and the campsite of Wood's division to their rear at the crossroads.[130]

Wheeler's men annoyed the Yankee pickets until about 9:00 P.M. that night, when they made a final charge before falling back to their own encampment. The next morning, however, the Rebels returned in force, and, at about 7 o'clock, they finally succeeded in overrunning the blue pickets at the creek. Charging into the Federal cavalry's camp, they captured many prisoners and horses and inflicted several casualties. Although a counterattack by a Union cavalry squadron drove them back across the creek, Wheeler's horsemen eventually regrouped and overran the Federal cavalry a second time, noisily driving them down the road toward the campsite of Woods's division.[131]

At this point, one of Woods's brigades came to the rescue. These infantrymen, already astir because of their orders to demonstrate toward Macon, were commanded by one of General Sherman's most trusted lieutenants, Brigadier General Charles C. Walcutt. It was he who in 1862 had carried out Sherman's orders to destroy the Tennessee town of Randolph, "leaving one house to mark the place."[132]

Walcutt threw forward a heavy line of skirmishers, supported by horse artillery. These troops surprised and repelled Wheeler's advance line and pushed back his reserve, running the Rebel cavalry across a frosty field and ultimately into and past the ruins of Griswoldville. By about 10:00 A.M. the cavalry skirmish was over. Despite their retreat, Wheeler's troopers had done well. With minimal losses they had inflicted seventy-five casualties on Kilpatrick and had ridden off with thirty-five horses as well.[133]

Familiar with Wheeler's tactics and persistence, corps commander Osterhaus expected still another cavalry attack. To protect his wagons from further interference, he ordered Walcutt's brigade to entrench in some mostly open land 1 1/2 miles east of Griswoldville, blocking a road that led directly to his route to Irwinton.[134]

## 16.
## DIGGING IN AT DUNCAN'S FARM

The site chosen for Walcutt's position was known locally as the Duncan farm, though Samuel Griswold had purchased it from Davis Duncan some fifteen years earlier. Since Griswold had acquired the acreage mainly as railroad property, the farmhouse was vacant and the fields neglected. But, unquestionably, the site offered excellent terrain for a defending force. The timbered ridge where the Yankees dug in looked toward Griswoldville across a wide, fallow field that rolled toward the railroad tracks. Below the ridge ran an overgrown branch, lined with small willow trees. This narrow watercourse, though marshy in places, also passed through some shallow gullies. From the near bank of the branch, the ground rose steeply for over one hundred yards to the top of the ridge. By occupying its crest, the Federals could block one of the two roads south of the tracks and command the other. At the same time, the position was difficult to turn since both of Walcutt's flanks rested near tangled swamps, with the right flank further strengthened by the railroad embankment.[135]

Just two miles to the rear of Walcutt's line, division headquarters occupied the summit of a steep hill on the Irwinton road, just one mile below

Captain A. F. R. Arndt, USA. Supposing himself mortally wounded, Arndt lay near his battery section during its destruction. (Burton Historical Collection, Detroit Public Library, Detroit, Michigan.)

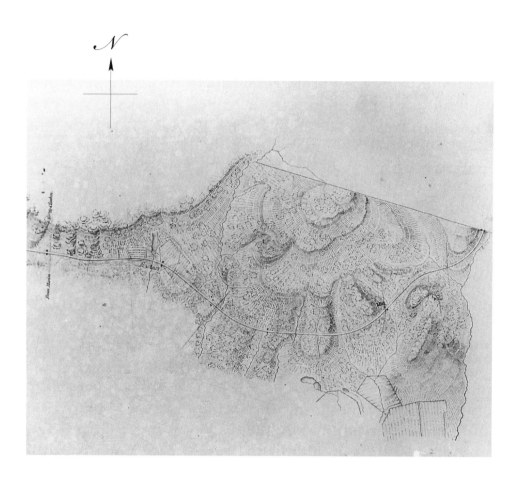

Duncan's Farm. The ridge on the farm is conspicuous in this antebellum map, drafted about a decade before the founding of Griswoldville. The ridge appears below and to the right of the 180-mile marker, from the vicinity of which "Battleline Branch" flows. The future site of Griswoldville is marked by the two squares on the rail line toward the center of the map, which represent the 181-mile marker from Savannah. (From *Thirteen Maps Shewing the Location of the Central Railroad of Georgia. Commenced November 1836. Completed November 1843. L. O. Reynolds, Engineer*, Georgia Historical Society.)

the rail line. The hilltop, site of Mountain Springs Church, had not seen so much activity since 1856, when three thousand people had gathered there to hear Alexander H. Stephens and other speakers. To strengthen this position the Federals dismantled the small church, making breast-works of its timbers and pews, and entrenched through a portion of the cemetery; additional breastworks were thrown up to the south. This base would serve as Walcutt's ammunition depot, and, if necessary, his field hospital.[136]

On the ridge at Duncan's Farm, Walcutt's men moved past rain-black-ened pine trunks to their positions. By early afternoon, the Union line was solidly in place. At the line's center, on the road to Mountain Springs, a battery section of two field pieces was emplaced in a crude lunette. To the left, three regiments, numbering 751 men (the 40th Illinois, the 100th Indiana, and the 46th Ohio), stretched toward swampy ground. Lightly entrenched behind makeshift breastworks, these infantrymen command-ed the road winding southeast from Griswoldville toward Irwinton. Three other regiments, totaling 762 men (the 6th Iowa, the 103d Illinois, and the 97th Indiana), stretched toward the other morass and the adjacent railway embankment; their line fronted the branch and field more exact-ly. Dug in behind stacked fence-rails, these soldiers had also partially torn down several log farm buildings that stood near the road. These structures' timbers had furnished additional material for the field fortifications, while the remaining foundations provided an array of outer works down the slope. If Wheeler's troopers attempted to use any of the roads running east from Griswoldville—or tried to travel cross-country over the Duncan farm—they would find reason to regret it.[137]

While they waited under the overcast sky, some of Walcutt's men ate hasty meals of hardtack, raw bacon, and hot coffee. As they bundled against the cold, a light sleet began to rattle into the pine straw at their feet. Then, at about 3:00 P.M., the men on the ridge heard rifle fire from the direction of Griswoldville. As the buglers sounded assembly, the Federals saw that their pickets were being driven across the field, and they realized with some consternation that this flight was not inspired by charging cavalry. Instead, it was obvious that a large body of enemy

The monument to Brigadier General Pleasant J. Philips in Linwood Cemetery, Columbus, Georgia. Philips and his wife had no children, and she remarried after his death; no likeness of him appears to have been handed down. Philips was colonel of the 31st Georgia until early 1862 when he resigned and was replaced by general-to-be Clement Anselm Evans. (Courtesy of the author.)

Captain Ruel W. Anderson, CSA. Anderson's battery prevented the defeat at Griswoldville from becoming a full-fledged disaster. A postwar photograph. (Courtesy of the Anderson family.)

Lieutenant Colonel Beverly D. Evans, Georgia State Line. Commander of the Georgia State Line, the most experienced infantrymen in Philips's force, Evans spent several harrowing hours below the ridge at Duncan's Farm. (Courtesy of the Evans family.)

infantry was massing across the field. The raw wind carried their Rebel yells clearly to the men behind the field works.[138]

An unfortunate chain of events had brought the Augusta-bound Georgia state troops into the Yankees' presence. The majority of Wheeler's cavalry, for whom this martial reception was intended, had left the area before noon. Striking southeast, the Rebel troopers intended to cross the Oconee River and reappear in front of Sherman's columns southeast of Milledgeville. The morning's skirmish had literally represented their parting shot, though this was unknown to Walcutt's men. Throughout the coming battle, they would anxiously await a cavalry attack.[139]

Like Wheeler and his men, Major General Gustavus Woodson Smith, commander of the Georgia Militia, was also absent from the Yankees' front. In the past, when combat was in the offing, he had sometimes suffered bouts of paralysis, apparently from an inability to tolerate the "mental excitement" of battle. Ostensibly, he had stayed behind in Macon to round up additional wagons and supplies. In any case, on the morning of 22 November he had sent his mixed force toward Griswoldville under the command of the militia's ranking brigadier general, Pleasant Jackson Philips. A former Columbus, Georgia, banker, Philips had served briefly in Virginia as a regimental commander earlier in the war but, on balance, he was the least experienced of the militia generals. His orders were to march his brigades to Griswoldville and wait there for further instructions.[140]

Attached to Philips's largely untried force were two groups of experienced soldiers: the Georgia State Line and Captain Ruel W. Anderson's battery of the 14th Georgia Light Artillery. The State Line, two under-strength regiments of conscription-age volunteers in state service, had begun as bridge guards on the Western and Atlantic Railroad. They had seen considerable combat during the Atlanta Campaign, while the militia had seldom left the "ditches." Totaling about 400, the men of the State Line were commanded by Lieutenant Colonel Beverly D. Evans. A veteran of the First Georgia Regiment (Ramsay's), he was a brother of Confederate Brigadier General Nathan G. "Shanks" Evans, of Bull Run and Ball's Bluff fame.[141]

But the most seasoned fighters present on the Southern side at Griswoldville were Anderson's Confederate artillerists, many of whom lived in nearby Pulaski County. They had fought numerous battles in Tennessee and Virginia, as well as in Georgia. The militiamen knew them well and valued them highly, since they had supported them during the fighting around Atlanta.[142]

## 17.
## ADVANCING TOWARD DISASTER

At about 8:00 A.M. on 22 November, General Philips had left Macon with his troops, some 1900 men all told. Most of them had camped overnight at the city fairgrounds. Miserably cold, some had resorted to ripping stairsteps from Macon buildings to feed their camp fires. Daylight had brought no warmth; the most vivid memory of one of the teenage militiamen who made the march would be his certainty that his hands had frozen to his musket. For his part, Philips fought the cold with draughts of liquor.[143]

Shivering, tired, and footsore, Philips's men reached a point one mile west of Griswoldville at about one in the afternoon. There they found Major F. W. C. Cook's Reserve battalions—some 400 men—drawn up in line of battle, facing the ruins of the village. An Englishman who owned a large armory in Athens, Cook commanded two units of mostly conscription-age soldiers. One of them was composed principally of his workmen, armed with the excellent Enfield-pattern rifles they manufactured. The other unit comprised employees of the Augusta powder works. Major George T. Jackson usually commanded them but had stepped aside

The Cook and Brother Armory, Athens, Georgia. F. W. C. Cook, an English-born industrialist, moved to Athens after the fall of New Orleans, constructed an impressive
armory, and soon began producing Enfield-pattern rifles. He organized a unit of
reserves, principally from his operatives, with himself as major. Though Cook survived
the Griswoldville battle, he was killed near Savannah by a Federal sharpshooter on 11
December 1864, and buried in the crypt of Stephen Elliott, Episcopal Bishop of Georgia,
in Savannah's Laurel Grove Cemetery. Confederate ordnance officer Colonel James H.
Burton said of Major Cook that he "exhibited a much better appreciation of the requirements of an armory than any other person who has attempted a like enterprise in the
Confederacy." The armory is shown as it appeared after the war. (Hargrett Rare Book
and Manuscript Library, University of Georgia Libraries.)

Private Harry Cook, Athens Battalion (23d Battalion of Cobb's Reserves), shown attired in a shell jacket. (Courtesy of David Wynn Vaughan.)

Private S. J. Baldwin, Georgia State Line. Born in 1850, Baldwin exemplified the unusually young men who were found among the state troops. He was not with his unit at Griswoldville, however, since one of his hands had been mangled months earlier at Kennesaw Mountain. In later years he received a Confederate disability pension of ten dollars per annum. (Kennesaw Mountain Battlefield National Park, Kennesaw, Georgia.)

Private A. J. Jackson, Second Regiment, Georgia State Line. Jackson was among those who charged across the open field toward the ridge at Duncan's Farm. As the Federals opened fire, he wrote, "the boys fell one after another. I ran some 30 or 40 yards and lay down by a stump and while lying there, I was struck on the arm, which caused me to lose the use of it. The bullets struck the stump and cut the ground on either side." Next, he continued, "some poor fellow fell down on me, wounded in both legs, trying to shelter himself behind the stump." When the retreat came later, the crippled soldier, like many others, had to be left where he lay. A postwar portrait. (Courtesy of Natalie Redfern.)

Brigadier General Henry Kent McCay, Georgia Militia. A native Pennsylvanian and graduate of Princeton, McCay (pronounced "McCoy") won fame as a lawyer before the war,
was a Confederate captain and militia brigadier during the conflict, and in the postbellum period served as an Associate Justice of the Georgia Supreme Court. (Georgia
Department of Archives and History.)

Brigadier General Charles D. Anderson, Georgia Militia. Like some other officers and men of the Georgia Militia, Anderson had seen service with the Army of Northern Virginia earlier in the war and had been discharged because of wounds, taken at such battles as Chancellorsville, where he "was severely wounded in the bowels and shoulder, and also lost a finger on his left hand." He said of his troops at Griswoldville, "After discharging the old men and cripples I had as good a brigade as was in the army, as its record will show." (Georgia Department of Archives and History.)

in favor of Cook. Major Cook and his men, who had also been ordered to Augusta by Hardee, had been in the vicinity when Wheeler's cavalry had been pushed through Griswoldville. Having notified Macon of the situation, Cook was awaiting orders.[144]

Cook's report had reached Macon just after noon and had greatly alarmed General Smith. He and Governor Brown had been warned by Lieutenant General Richard Taylor—who had arrived in Macon just after the militia's departure—that the state troops were probably on a collision course with some of Sherman's troops. Immediately, a courier was sent galloping toward Griswoldville to retrieve Philips and his men.[145]

At about the time the order was dispatched, General Philips was embarking on an adventure. Seeing a dense column of smoke billowing from the village (and believing from reports of straggling cavalry that the enemy was numerically inferior to his force), he threw out the State Line troops in a heavy skirmish line and advanced toward Griswoldville with his and Cook's men. Encountering no opposition, Philips's force entered the ruined village and discovered the source of the smoke: the Griswold barn had been set afire by the Yankees. Philips consulted further with Cook and decided to march along the railroad to a point east of the ruins to await further orders. Cook determined to continue marching eastward, hoping to make connection with his rail transport to Augusta. His units marched on ahead of the militia.[146]

Cook's skirmishers encountered Walcutt's pickets even before the militia column had cleared the smoldering rubble of Griswoldville. With the bulk of his force screened from the Federals by a stand of pines, Philips rode to the edge of the open field. There Cook showed him the enemy position on the ridge opposite them. Deciding to attack, Philips ordered his subordinates to bring their men into line of battle.[147]

North of the railroad, near an abandoned railroad station house one mile east of Griswoldville, Anderson's batterymen unlimbered their four twelve-pounder Napoleons and brought them into position. Assuming decisive numerical superiority—and probably emboldened by the support of the experienced Confederate artillerists—Philips ordered an assault along the enemy's entire front. Since they had gone into position first,

Cook's Athens and Augusta Battalions were to hit Walcutt's left. Next to arrive, Lieutenant Colonel Evans's State Line regiments and Brigadier General Henry Kent McCay's Fourth Militia Brigade were to strike the enemy's center. Brigadier General Charles D. Anderson's Third Militia Brigade was hurried into a field north of the tracks to be sent against the Federal right, while Philips's own Second Militia Brigade, commanded by Colonel James N. Mann of Morgan County, was directed to remain in reserve. In almost every case, Philips's orders were garbled in transmission or simply misunderstood, for from the start the attack was fatally uncoordinated. Its progress could only be observed by General Smith's courier, who arrived from Macon just as the battle opened, too late for the role of savior.[148]

## 18.
## THE BATTLE OF GRISWOLDVILLE

When the first Rebels advanced into the bare field, supported by fire from Anderson's battery, Federal shells came screaming toward the tracks and inflicted some casualties among Cook's men. The Confederate Napoleons, however, wreaked considerably more havoc: one of the first shells damaged a caisson, and succeeding shots prevented the Union cannoneers from inflicting much damage on the charging Rebel infantrymen or their artillery support. As the cannonades began, musket fire dropped Captain A. F. R. Arndt, commander of the Federal battery. Since a shot had pierced his "overcoat, blouse, and vest," Arndt "could not think otherwise than that the ball had passed straight through [his] body." By the time that he realized he had only been bruised by a spent bullet, several shells had plunged into his position and exploded "in all directions around [him]." As the captain got to his feet, there was no mistaking the actual

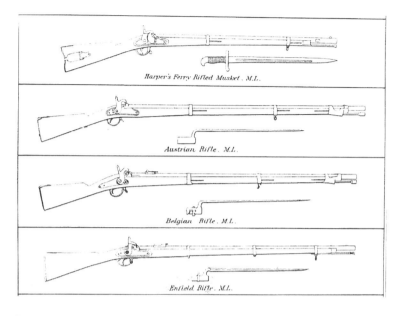

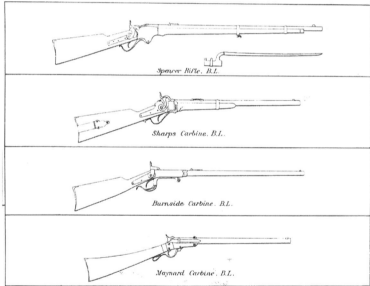

Muzzleloaders, Breechloaders, and Repeaters. The superiority of Federal shoulder arms is apparent in these engravings from the first edition of *The Atlas to Accompany the Official Records of the Union and Confederate Armies* (1891-1895). The Confederate weapons (above) were muzzleloaders requiring ramrods. Federal carbines and rifles (below) ranged from the much more convenient breech-loaders to the technological marvel of the Spencer repeater, conspicuously used at Griswoldville. The Spencer featured a tubular magazine that loaded through the buttstock and contained seven shells for rapid fire—with cartridge boxes holding up to thirteen additional magazines. (Hargrett Rare Book and Manuscript Library, University of Georgia Libraries.)

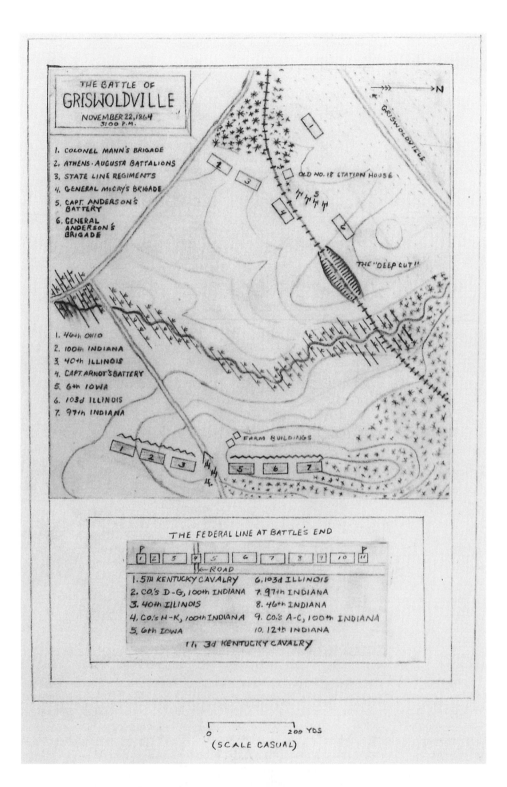

The Battle of Griswoldville. (Author's collection)

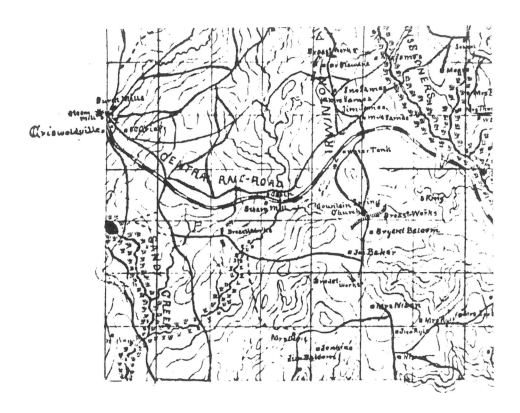

The Griswoldville Battlefield. This detail from "Map of the 6th District of Jones Co." shows the location of the Federal breastworks. (National Archives.)

carnage among his men and horses. Several of his batterymen had been dismembered by shells, and six of his horses lay slaughtered. To save their guns, the remaining artillerists had to pull them to safety by their prolonges.[149]

As the disjointed Rebel lines rushed across the field at "double quick," the Yankee rifles remained silent. The Rebels seemed fearless—and were certainly noisy. One Federal later recalled that he never heard the "Rebel yell" more loudly than at the Battle of Griswoldville. Philips's men made their way across the field, bayonets fixed, flags aloft—hoping to push the enemy from his works. Then, as the Rebel troops began their descent toward the branch below the ridge, they finally heard the rattle of rifle fire from the Federal line. The air suddenly came alive, as bullets plucked at the flags and tore through clothing and flesh. Immediately, the Rebels' ranks began to thin under the volleys of the Yankee repeaters. Those who could manage it took advantage of the concealment offered by the undergrowth along the branch and of the protection of the gullies through which it ran. Others failed to make it and lay motionless or writhing in the field.[150]

Before reaching the branch, the advance line of Rebels—principally the State Line, supported to the right by Cook's battalions—stopped to fire, then jumped or splashed to the other side of the branch and started up the slope, where they delivered another volley. This unexpected rush uphill, and the volley that accompanied it, succeeded in driving those Federals in the wrecked cabins back behind their main breastworks. At this point, an astonished Evans realized that his men were taking fire from the rear as well as their front. Some of McCay's militiamen had just arrived in the thickets along the stream, and—disoriented by the smoke and disarray—had fired toward Evans's men, mistaking them for the enemy. The State Line fell back in confusion, with one regiment following some of Anderson's militiamen, who had been ordered "to move by the left flank." Though the State Line regiment's movement toward the left had created a gap in the line, it was promptly filled by militiamen. In fact, the entire militia force soon clustered below the ridge, for the reserve brigade under

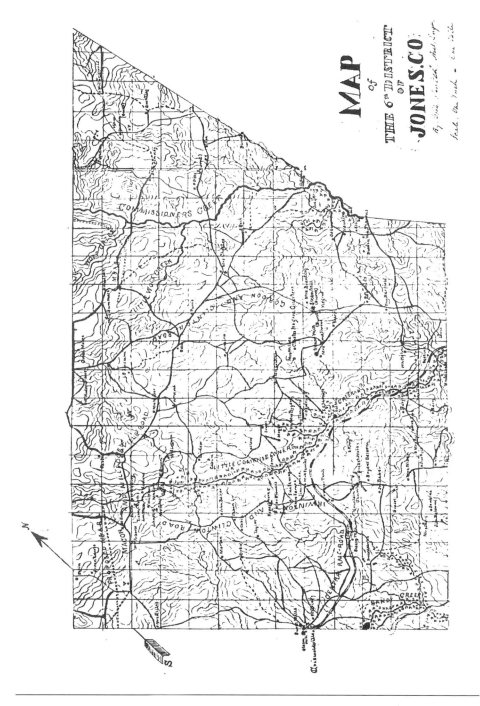

"Map of the 6th District of Jones Co." This map and the one following were traced by Federal field cartographers from maps removed from the Jones County Courthouse in Clinton. Both include notations of dwellings and other property burned, together with identifications of property owners. The original courthouse maps have not survived. (National Archives.)

"Map of the 9th District of Jones Co." (National Archives.)

Colonel Mann had unaccountably made its way into the teeming branch.[151]

The State Line, the militia, and Cook's men were now mingled regardless of unit among the briers, gall bushes, and cane. Their predicament was extremely dangerous, seemingly hopeless. Armed with muzzleloaders, the Rebels occupied a position that made reloading difficult and accurate fire almost impossible. Mostly raw, these troops faced an experienced, battle-hardened enemy, many armed with seven-shot Spencer repeating rifles and occupying a fortified height. The Yankees' fire, obstructed only intermittently by rises in the slope, was rapid and accurate; it poured into the willow thickets along the branch, tearing through leaves, clipping off branches, and sometimes cutting into flesh and bone. The Yankee riflemen, moreover, could depend upon being resupplied with ammunition and could also be reinforced if necessary—two luxuries denied to Philips's men.[152]

The Rebels' alternatives were strictly limited. A retreat back across the open field would have been suicidal, if not dishonorable. Lateral movement was blocked by the flanking swamps and the Federals posted there. The only way out of this predicament, it seemed, was frontal attack—though that seemed likely to lead to annihilation. Yet attack they did, at least three times, though each time heavy fire hurled them back down the slope into the overgrown branch.[153]

Mercifully, sundown came early in November. By 5:00 P.M. visibility had greatly decreased. An hour later, darkness ended the Rebels' ordeal, and the badly mauled troops retired toward Griswoldville. Nonetheless, they made their escape at the painful cost of leaving behind many of their wounded and dying, along with all of their dead. The Griswolds opened their house to those wounded who could be brought back. Some would prove to be too badly hurt to be moved again for some time. Among those who would survive were Lieutenant Colonel Evans and Colonel Mann.[154]

General Philips intended to camp near Griswoldville and send detachments back to the battlefield to retrieve as many of the wounded and dead as possible. But orders awaited him to return to Macon, where there had been another alarm (again false) of an enemy attack. The railroad had now

The Griswoldville Battlefield, Looking toward the Ridge. A 1980 photograph. (Courtesy of the author. Photography by Tammy Thompson.)

been repaired some distance past Macon, and boxcars had been sent as far as possible, accompanied by Dr. T. A. Raines, the militia's chief surgeon. By 2:00 A.M. on 23 November, Philips and his men were back in Macon, where some of the wounded would soon be transported to hospitals as far west as Columbus.[155]

## 19.
## THE VIEW FROM THE RIDGE

The Federals on the ridge at Duncan's Farm had not escaped the battle unscathed, but most of their casualties were to the credit of the Rebel cannoneers, not the infantrymen. The shells from Anderson's battery had not only silenced the Yankee cannons but had also crashed frequently into the rail and log breastworks on the ridge's crest, throwing deadly shrapnel and splinters along the blue line. In mid-battle a shell fragment had, in fact, ripped deeply into General Walcutt's right calf, sending him to the rear, whereupon Colonel R. F. Catterson of the 97th Indiana Infantry had taken command. The Rebel artillery also crippled or killed many of the mules that were drawing ammunition wagons to the Federals. In one of the battle's grisliest moments, a "single shell [had] struck and exploded in the rail and log barricade where the regimental colors [of the Sixth Iowa] were waving," killing the color bearer by "blowing the top of his head off and saturating the colors with his blood."[156]

Even the hapless Rebel infantry had given the Federals some cause for anxiety—quite aside from the fact that their superior numbers and their several charges up the slope had disturbed some of Walcutt's men. For almost the entire battle, the Yankee line had been most dangerously threatened to the right, and Walcutt had continuously weakened his left to strengthen and extend the endangered section of his line. At one point, pressure to the right was so sustained that it seemed a bayonet offensive might be necessary. The threat eased, but near the end of the battle, field commander Catterson was disagreeably surprised to learn that there had again been a massive push against his right. This new menace came from a portion of General Anderson's militia brigade, which had belatedly entered the fray. When their line had swept across the tracks toward the field, a portion had been blocked by a deep railway cut. Anderson—having had two horses shot from under him and having been severely wounded in one hand—had ultimately led these men from their position and directed them in this vigorous and unexpected assault. Catterson consequently shifted even more men to the right and called for reinforcements. He received an additional infantry regiment for the right, as well as squadrons of Kilpatrick's cavalry for both flanks.[157]

In general, however, Philips's reckless attack had elicited more Yankee derision than alarm. One account tells of catcalls and hoots directed at the charging Rebels, of dares thrown down to the branch for more charges. But when the Union skirmishers moved down from the ridge after dark, their amusement gave way to a remorse unusual in such seasoned veterans. For on the slopes, in the branch and its thickets, and in the field beyond, they discovered that a large number of the dead, wounded, and dying were the young boys and elderly men of the Georgia Militia. "Old gray-haired men and weakly looking men and little boys not over fifteen years old lay dead or writhing in pain," wrote one Federal officer. "I hope that we will never have to shoot at such men again." Another Federal officer discovered a particularly horrific scene: a badly wounded teenage boy surrounded by the corpses of his father, two brothers, and an uncle.[158]

Amazingly, however, though the Federals had wounded almost five hundred of their opponents, the Rebel dead on the field numbered only about fifty. Those killed, however, included several officers such as Colonel Abner F. Redding of Jones County, commander of the Seventh Regiment, Third Brigade, Georgia Militia, "loved to idolatry by his men," and Captains M. L. Curry, Arch Pittman and E. F. Strozier. Of the wounded left on the field, those who could be moved were taken to the

The Jones County Courthouse, Clinton. This view, which shows the structure when abandoned after removal of the county seat in the early 1900s, approximates the building's condition after the events of late November 1864. (Georgia Department of Archives and History.)

The Deep Cut, Looking toward the Battlefield. A 1980 photograph. (Courtesy of the author. Photography by Tammy Thompson.)

rear as prisoners. The badly hurt were made as comfortable as conditions allowed—and provided with full canteens and blankets—but were left where they fell. Predictably, several died of exposure during the bitterly cold night.[159]

Although the Yankees had suffered over one hundred casualties, only about a dozen men had been killed. They were wrapped in their blankets and buried on the field of action, some with wooden headboards to mark their graves. By nine that evening activity on Duncan's Farm had all but ceased. As one Union soldier described it, the afternoon's "incessant roar of artillery and musketry…the loud yelling and cheering of the men" gave place to the "mournful sighing of the wind among the pines and the pitiable moans of the wounded and dying."[160]

## 20.
## THE REASONS WHY

The reasons for such a fiasco are numerous. Philips was certainly blameworthy. His relative inexperience had been fatally compounded by inebriation and disobedience of orders. He would soon be blamed for the defeat by General Smith and replaced by Colonel Dexter Booth Thompson, also of Columbus. In a memorandum to Adjutant General Wayne, General Smith would argue strongly for the creation of a permanent examining board and court martial for the Georgia Militia. He felt that all the militia officers should all be examined as to qualifications and "when found incompetent should be reduced to the ranks."[161]

But the role of Philips alone did not entirely explain the disaster. There were other factors, related to the large component of militiamen in the Rebel force. Many of these citizen-soldiers were local men from Bibb, Wilkinson, Jones, and Putnam Counties. As such, they had more than an ordinary sense of outrage at an enemy pillaging and burning in their midst, seemingly with impunity. In the semi-democratic command structure that was characteristic even of the Confederate army, the militia's "spoiling for a fight" may have influenced the decision to attack. "Where the battle had raged fiercely," wrote one Union memoirist, "and the enemy had made a desperate stand, in the midst of a large number of dead and dying men, was found a modest-appearing countryman, with gray beard, who exhibited under his coarse shirt a mortal wound in his breast and then, making a feeble gesture with his hand, said: 'My neighborhood is ruined, these people are all my neighbors.'"[162]

Also, the men of the militia seem to have felt a need to prove their worth as soldiers, since by this point in the war they had received steadier fire from the press, public opinion, and their Confederate counterparts than they had from the enemy. Long derided as "Joe Brown's Pets," they had recently been mocked in the newspapers over their "agricultural leave." And they had even had to endure being lampooned in a popular ditty: "Just before the battle the General hears a row,/ He says, 'The Yanks are coming, I hear their rifles now.'/ He turns around in wonder, and what do you thinks he sees?/ The Georgia Militia, eating goober peas!" With unconscious prophecy, Howell Cobb had written earlier of such soldiers, "They dread the jeers and sneers which they must encounter… more than they do the bullets of the Yankees."[163]

Indeed, soon after the battle, an irate militiaman would demand that a Macon newspaper clarify a published report that had named Wheeler's cavalry as the Rebel force at the Battle of Griswoldville. "Wheeler's cavalry had nothing to do with it," the offended citizen-soldier wrote. It was, he explained, the militia that "had had the honor of the fight." That force, he added, contained "good fighting stock, though much ridiculed." A Federal writer seemed to agree with this assessment. The militiamen were out to prove something, he thought, for they "did not immediately give way, but seemed to show fight, as much as to say, 'We'll show you that militia can fight.'"[164]

Four other Federal soldiers summed up the range of opinion among the victors as they reflected on the battle. One attributed the attack to the

Private P. C. Key, Georgia Militia. Like some militiamen, Key had served in the Georgia State Guard for six months in 1863 and 1864. Said to have been a descendant of Francis Scott Key, he died charging against a descendant of the Star-Spangled Banner at Griswoldville. (Georgia Department of Archives and History.)

# REPORTS

OF THE

## OPERATIONS OF THE MILITIA,

FROM OCTOBER 13, 1864, TO FEBRUARY 11, 1865,

BY

MAJ.-GENERALS G. W. SMITH AND WAYNE,

TOGETHER WITH

## MEMORANDA BY GEN. SMITH,

FOR THE

## IMPROVEMENT OF THE STATE MILITARY ORGANIZATION.

MACON, GA.

BOUGHTON, NESBIT, BARNES & MOORE,
State Printers.

---

*Reports of the Operations of the Militia* (1865). This wartime publication collected the official reports of the 1st Division, Georgia Militia, during the March to the Sea. It was printed at Macon, then Georgia's de facto capital because of disarray in recently-occupied Milledgeville. (Special Collections Library, Duke University, Durham, North Carolina)

Engraved by A.B. Walter, Phila.

General P. G. T. Beauregard, CSA. Newly named commander of the Confederacy's Military Division of the West—which stretched from Georgia to Mississippi— Beauregard presided over Hood's fiasco in Tennessee, as well as the futile resistance to Sherman's March. He added to the heavy weight of brass in Macon by arriving on 24 November, after the crisis was past. (Hargrett Rare Book and Manuscript Library, University of Georgia Libraries.)

"ignorance of danger common to new troops," while another felt that the militiamen "knew nothing at all about fighting and...their officers knew as little." The third wrote admiringly that during Sherman's subsequent march through the Carolinas, no Rebels from Savannah to Fayetteville had shown as much "pluck" as the Georgia Militia at Griswoldville. But the last observer was simply appalled. Viewing the carnage, he sadly characterized it as a "harvest of death."[165]

Whatever the reason for the disaster, its significance was aptly described by Georgia historian Charles C. Jones, Jr., himself a Confederate officer during the Savannah Campaign. For his book on the March to the Sea, Jones corresponded with several of the Rebel officers and men who had fought in the battle, as well as others indirectly involved, and based his conclusions on their accounts. "The Battle of Griswoldville," he wrote, "will be remembered as an unfortunate accident whose occurrence might have been avoided by the exercise of proper caution and circumspection. It in no wise crippled the enemy and entailed upon the Confederates a loss which, under the circumstances, could be illy sustained." More briefly, he called the battle "unnecessary, unexpected, and utterly unproductive of any good."[166]

Lieutenant Colonel Charles C. Jones, Jr., CSA. Mayor of Savannah when war broke out, Jones soon took his post as an officer of the Chatham Artillery; he served as Hardee's Chief of Artillery during the Siege of Savannah. Several years after the war, Jones determined to write an account of the Savannah Campaign. "As yet," he noted, "the history of those operations has been written only by those who gloated over our reverses, and made sport of our calamities." Corresponding extensively with Confederate veterans of the campaign, he produced a classic with a ponderous title: *The Siege of Savannah in December, 1864, and the Confederate Operations in Georgia and the Third Military District of South Carolina during General Sherman's March from Atlanta to the Sea* (1874). His own abundantly extra-illustrated copy of his book, found in the Hargrett Library, provided several illustrations for this book. (Special Collections Library, Duke University.)

Brigadier General Reuben W. Carswell, Georgia Militia. Carswell rose to the lieutenant colonelcy of the 48th Georgia, but Senator Herschel V. Johnson proposed to President Davis that this officer "of fine talents" be given his own regiment. Instead, he was disabled by an arm wound at Gettysburg and returned to Georgia. There he served in the legislature before being elected brigadier general in early June 1864 to command the first brigade of militia to be organized in the 1st Division. During the March to the Sea, his brigade was commanded by Colonel J. T. Willis. At war's end in Augusta, Carswell witnessed the spectacle of Governor Brown collapsing in tears at the thought of being tried for treason. (Courtesy of C. D. Lester.)

## 21.

## AFTERMATH

The battle over, the Union victors departed, leaving behind them an eerie "stillness," with a people beginning to absorb "the sense of ruin which was upon them with their cotton destroyed," with "all their stores for the winter pillaged," and their animals and livestock slaughtered or "driven off." Walcutt's men had won what would prove to be the only major infantry battle of the Savannah Campaign. Howard's stratagem for the battle, like Sherman's for the campaign, had succeeded wonderfully well: the last of the Federal right wing's supply, pontoon, and ammunition wagons rumbled into safety near Gordon on 24 November, finally free from mud, ice, and danger.[167]

When the march resumed, General Walcutt had to ride seaward in a carriage, and would not return to command his brigade for several months. But he was no doubt cheered by his post-battle brevet to major general, a reward for "special gallantry." Kilpatrick—whose wanton destructiveness was already earning him a place in Southern demonology—left Middle Georgia outraged over reports that some of Wheeler's men had cut the throats of several captured Yankee cavalrymen. He and Wheeler were destined to clash again before the campaign ended.[168]

Ironically, the state troops would be given an opportunity to exact a certain amount of vengeance for having been so soundly whipped at the Battle of Griswoldville (or of Duncan's Farm, as some would have it). Rejoined by Carswell's First Brigade (apparently after adventures of its own), the militiamen were reunited with General Smith. Under his command they were sent to help defend Savannah, now obviously the Yankees' actual target. After a train ride broken by a long forced march between unconnected stations, Carswell's brigade, together with the State Line and Cook's battalions, arrived in Savannah. There General Hardee ordered them to proceed at once into South Carolina, where a Federal force was threatening to cut the railroad above Savannah and isolate it from Charleston and Richmond.[169]

It took much persuasion to convince General Smith and his men to leave the state they had been mustered to defend, but leave they did—and were well rewarded for it. Outside Grahamville, South Carolina, on 30 November 1864, Smith's troops—under the command of a local Confederate officer, Colonel Charles J. Colcock, occupied a low, fortified ridge known as Honey Hill. Repeated Yankee attacks did not budge them, and the battle ended as an almost perfect reversal of the Battle of Griswoldville. Smith's 1400 infantrymen suffered a mere fifty casualties, only eight of them deaths. The Union commander, however, lost over 750 men of his 5500-man force, almost ninety of whom were killed. The Rebel triumph bought time for Hardee to evacuate safely the mere 10,000 men he had been able to gather in Savannah's defense. As a minor victory in a futile campaign, the Battle of Honey Hill would be all but lost to history. But to Carswell's Brigade of "Joe Brown's Pets," the engagement "wiped out the stain" of the earlier encounter and avenged in part the beating their comrades had taken on the slopes beyond Griswoldville.[170]

After Sherman captured Savannah (and abandoned it to march through the Carolinas), the Georgia Militia, the Georgia State Line, and Cobb's Reserves spent most of the rest of the war on garrison duty—though some would participate in the final battle fought on Georgia soil. At Columbus, Brigadier General James Harrison Wilson's "Yankee blitzkrieg" rolled across the Chattahoochee and routed the town's defenders. Their retreating commander, Howell Cobb, barely beat Wilson's men to Macon, which was taken and occupied after trifling casualties. Emptied of Federal prisoners, the Camp Oglethorpe stockade now briefly held surrendered Confederate and Georgia state soldiers. By the time Confederate president Jefferson Davis was brought prisoner to Macon in May 1865, the town had returned to a semblance of peace and order. But, unfortunately, one of the few fires that broke out during the Federal occupation of Macon destroyed most of the records of the Georgia Militia, helping make that unique organization an obscurity to future generations.[171]

Macon had survived almost intact. So had Prattville, whose gin factory continued in operation long after its founder's death in 1873. And Clinton, though sparsely populated, lived on as well, transformed into a quiet, rustic sanctuary ornamented with its surviving antebellum homes. But the story was much different at Griswoldville. There, Samuel Griswold's mansion had been spared, but it presided over ruins of

Brigadier General James H. Wilson, USA. Leading over 13,000 cavalrymen, Wilson tore through the last stronghold of the Confederacy, destroying or capturing major components of Southern war machinery from Selma, Alabama, to Macon, Georgia. On 7 May 1865, Governor Brown surrendered the Georgia Militia and the Georgia State Line to Wilson in Macon. (Massachusetts Commandery, Military Order of the Loyal Legion and the US Military History Institute.)

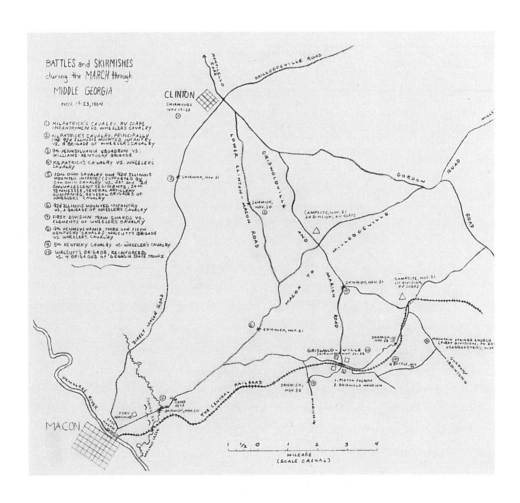

Middle Georgia during the March to the Sea. (Courtesy of the author.)

tumbled brick, twisted wreckage, and blackened timbers. Ironically, Griswold was not devastated by the sight. In fact, he almost took pleasure in the Federals' thorough and efficient destruction of "his life's work," for, "being thorough-going himself, he could appreciate it in others." Characteristically, he vowed that if he "could call back ten years," he would start anew and "soon make it all back." But, given his "advanced age and feeble health," Griswold instead went into complete retirement, well-earned after a half-century of remarkable achievement in his adopted state. Though his partner Arvin Gunnison's last-ditch attempt to restore the operations of the pistol factory had come to nothing, the total number of pistols produced stood very honorably at almost 3700—"more than any other manufacturer in the Confederacy and nearly as many as all other manufacturers combined."[172]

In his last days, Samuel Griswold made one more interesting purchase: Lowther Hall, into which his son-in-law Richard Wyatt Bonner moved with Griswold's grandchildren. Griswold sold some property as well. With the help of son-in-law E. C. Grier, Griswold in December 1865 disposed of his lands in lower Jones County and adjoining Twiggs, selling to Anthony Maxwell for $30,000 over 11,000 acres. Though this included the site of Griswoldville, it was arranged for Griswold to continue to live in his house, almost all that was left of his village. There, on 14 September 1867, died "this well-known gentleman"—as his obituary termed him—to be followed within three years by his wife. Both were buried in the Clinton cemetery, where their graves were marked by large stone monuments.[173]

Eventually, Griswold's village slowly returned to life. By 1900 it boasted around eighty inhabitants and again had a post office and a few stores. Somewhat later it would serve as the location for a public school. But Griswoldville was no longer an industrial community—only a rural hamlet—though distinguished for many years by the lofty brick chimney of the old pistol factory. Around a century after Samuel Griswold bought the land for its timber, a Kraft conglomerate did the same, and most surviving structures near the tracks were removed. By the centenary of the battle, Griswoldville had become little more than a name—an empty crossroads, dotted here and there with historical markers.

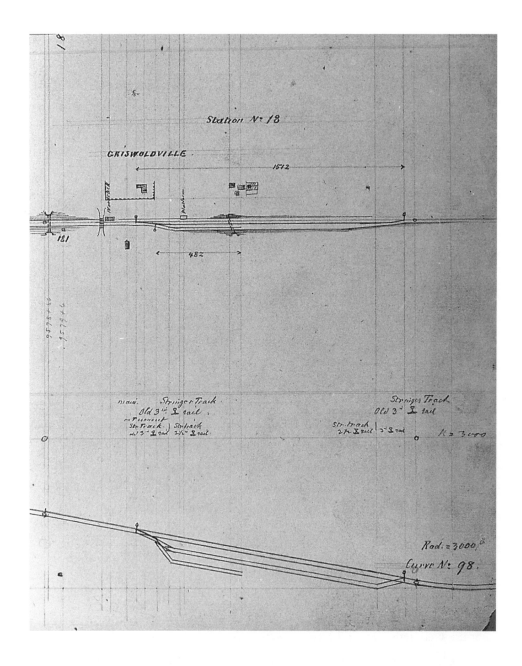

Griswoldville, 1866. This unusual diagram of Griswoldville, drafted the year after the war, places the south at the top. Adjacent to the 181 Mile Post is the culvert for the mill pond creek, with a culvert for another creek beneath the main line and the siding. Although the platform and wood rack are labeled, the other symbols are subject to speculation. (From Augustus Schwaab's *Diagram of Central RR Showing Location of Depots, Bridges, Buildings, Etc.* [1866], Georgia Historical Society.)

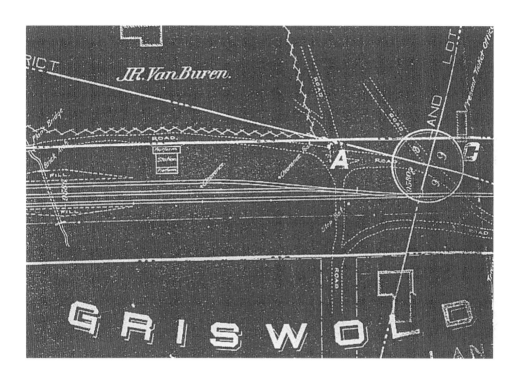

The heart of Griswoldville in 1900. This map shows Griswoldville's location near the intersection of the 8th and 9th Land Lots of the 6th and 7th Jones County Land Districts. The simple platform of 1866 has been replaced by a depot with two platforms, located between the Macon-Gordon Road and the tracks. The Van Buren house is in the vicinity of the obliterated pistol works, and the Griswold house appears above the "L" in "GRISWOLD." This is apparently its configuration; it soon burned, and later right-of-way diagrams show a square structure. (Box 6, Right of Way Files, Collection No. 1362AN-65, Georgia Historical Society.)

Jones County Confederate Veterans, c.1910. Presumably some of these old warriors saw the surrender at Stoneman's Hill or charged toward the ridge at Duncan's Farm. In the background is the Jones County Courthouse, built after the transfer of the county seat from Clinton to Gray in 1905. (Courtesy of the author.)

[1] Kenneth Coleman and Charles Stephen Gurr, eds., *Dictionary of Georgia Biography*, 2 vols. (Athens GA, 1983) 1:370 (Hereafter cited as *DGB*); William Lamar Cawthon, Jr., "Clinton: County Seat on the Georgia Frontier, 1808-1821" (M.A. thesis, University of Georgia, 1984) 17.

[2] Cawthon, "Clinton," 5, 45; James C. Bonner, *Milledgeville: Georgia's Antebellum Capital* (Athens GA, 1978) 21, 36.

[3] Cawthon, "Clinton," 59, 56; Old Clinton Historical Society, *An Historical Guide to Clinton, Georgia, An Early Nineteenth Century County Seat* (n.p., 1975) 3, 7; Cawthon, "Clinton," 33, 145; Deed Book P, 314, Office of the Clerk of the Superior Court, Jones County Courthouse, Gray, Georgia (All deed book citations are to this location); Ellen Griswold Hardeman, Manuscript Memoir of Samuel Griswold, in private possession (Samuel Griswold was grandfather of Mrs. Hardeman, who was the daughter of Griswold's daughter Mary Spencer Griswold Smith); Carolyn White Williams, *History of Jones County, Georgia* (Macon GA, 1957) 401; *Macon Telegraph*, 8 March 1890.

[4] *DGB*, 1:370; S. H. Griswold, "The Cotton Gin," *Jones County News*, 2 April 1908; Cawthon, "Clinton," 88, 189; Deed Book L, 26, and Deed Book M, 359. S. H. Griswold (1844-1917) was the son of Samuel Griswold's second son, Elisha Case Griswold. He worked for a time at the pistol works at Griswoldville and was also a member of the Georgia Militia, though he was not involved in the battle near his grandfather's village in late 1864. His series of lively articles for the *Jones County News*, which appeared in 1908 and 1909, are a major source for the history of Jones County in the 1800s and early 1900s. Available on microfilm, they are also conveniently collected, as photocopies, in volume four of Walter W. Spengler's and Bruce G. Spengler's extensive compilation *Griswoldville: A Collection of Maps, Pictures, Stories, and Personal Comments about the Man, the Town, the Battle, the Family*, copies of which are held by the Genealogical & Historical Room of the Washington Memorial Library, Macon, Georgia, and the Hargrett Library, University of Georgia Libraries, Athens.

[5] Griswold, "The Cotton Gin"; Deed Book N, 79, 144; James L. Watkins, *King Cotton: A Historical and Statistical Review, 1790-1908* (New York, 1908) 101; *Georgia Journal* (Milledgeville), 3 September 1827 and 14 July 1828.

[6] Deed Book O, 407; *DGB*, 1:370; *Historical Guide*, 10; Griswold, "The Cotton Gin."

[7] Griswold, "The Cotton Gin"; Karen Gerhardt Britton, *Bale o' Cotton: The Mechanical Art of Cotton Ginning* (College Station TX, 1992) 18; S. H. Griswold, "The Old Way of Ginning," *Jones County News*, 10 June 1909.

[8] Griswold, "The Cotton Gin"; Charles A. Bennett, *Saw and Toothed Cotton Ginning Developments* (Dallas TX, ca. 1960) 30, 36, 78; David W. Lewis, *Transactions of the Southern Central Agricultural Society* (Macon GA, 1852) 14-15; Geoffrey Tweedale,

*Sheffield Steel and America: A Century of Commercial and Technological Interdependence, 1830-1930* (Cambridge MA, 1987) 1-2, 7, 193n.42.

[9] Griswold, "The Cotton Gin"; Deed Book N, 135, 230, and Deed Book P, 60, 166, 522; Williams, *History of Jones County*, 226, 418; Merrill E. Pratt, *Daniel Pratt: Alabama's First Industrialist* (Birmingham AL, 1949) 12-15; Mrs. S. F. H. Tarrant, ed., *Hon. Daniel Pratt: A Biography* (Richmond VA, 1904) 21, 61; Britton, *Bale o' Cotton*, 33-34. Pratt also ran a textile mill at Prattville that produced Osnaburgs for clothing slaves (*De Bow's Review* [September 1846]: 153).

[10] Deed Book P, 142; *Southern Recorder* (Milledgeville), 17 July 1849.

[11] George White, *Statistics of the State of Georgia* (Savannah GA, 1849) 355; *Historical Guide*, 9-10; U. B. Phillips, *A History of Transportation in the Eastern Cotton Belt to 1860* (New York, 1908) 257; Griswold, "The Cotton Gin"; Deed Books Q and Deed Book R, various locations.

[12] Samuel Griswold, Depredation Affidavit, 11 February 1865 (typescript in private possession); US War Department, *War of the Rebellion: A Compilation of the Official Records of the Union and Confederate Armies*, 128 vols. (Washington, 1880-1901) [hereafter cited as *Official Records*; all citations are to Series 1, unless otherwise indicated; page number follows volume number], 44:368; US Census Office, Manuscript 1850 & 1860 Census, Slave Schedules, Jones County, Georgia (microfilm); Hardeman Memoir. Griswold's steam mill at the site of Griswoldville was in use as early as 12 February 1850, when a report submitted to the Jones County Inferior Court recommended that a new road be cut to the mill (County Affairs, 1842-1888, p. 261, Jones County Probate Court).

[13] Hardeman Memoir; Thomas Jefferson Stewart (1822-1902) Diary, 1860 [hereafter cited as Stewart Diary], Georgia Department of Archives and History, Atlanta, Georgia [hereafter cited as GDAH], various locations; Samuel Griswold to Merrit Camp, 25 October 1854 [hereafter cited as Samuel Griswold Letter], Miscellaneous File #481, GDAH; S. H. Griswold, "Benjamin James, His Sons, and What They Accomplished," *Jones County News*, 15 April 1909.

NOTE: Accompanying the Griswold letter cited above is a manuscript note speculating that Gunnison provided the slave force used to manufacture the Griswold & Gunnison revolvers, since Samuel Griswold "sold all his slaves on February 16, 1860." Griswold did indeed sell slaves on that date, but only two, both named Nancy (Deed Book S, 239).

[14] Augustus Schwaab, *Diagram of Central RR Showing Location of Depots, Bridges, Buildings, Etc.* (1866) Book 1, p. 80, #1362FA-90/42-D-3, Georgia Historical Society, Savannah, Georgia [location hereafter cited as GHS]; Ben H. McClary and LeRoy P. Graf, eds., "'Vineland' in Tennessee, 1852: The Journal of Rosine Parmentier," *The East Tennessee Historical Society's Publications* (No. 31, 1959):101; *Southern Recorder*, 8 March 1853; *Official Records*, 44:367.

[15] Joseph T. Derry, "A Condensed History," *Eighth Annual Report of the Commissioner of Commerce and Labor of the State of Georgia* (Atlanta, 1929) 22.

[16] US Census Office, Manuscript 1860 Census of Population, Jones County, Georgia (microfilm); Deed Book Q and Deed Book R, various locations; Williams, *History of Jones County*, 402-403; *Historical Guide*, 10.

[178] Joseph C. G. Kennedy, ed., *Population of the United States in 1860* (Washington, DC, 1864) 72-73; Stewart Diary, various locations.

[18] Hardeman Memoir; Griswold, "The Cotton Gin."

[19] William A. Albaugh III and Edward N. Simmons, *Confederate Arms* (Harrisburg, Pennsylvania, 1957) 123-131; Rodney Hilton Brown, *American Polearms* (New Milford, Connecticut, 1967) 125-134; Joseph H. Parks, *Joseph E. Brown of Georgia* (Baton Rouge LA, 1977) 242.

[20] William A. Albaugh III, *Confederate Edged Weapons* (New York, 1960) 54-56. These were apparently the only edged weapons produced at Griswoldville. Griswold swords, though sometimes attributed to Samuel Griswold, were actually produced by Thomas Griswold & Company of New Orleans (Albaugh and Simmons, *Confederate Arms*, 268-69).

[21] Pratt, *Daniel Pratt*, 18-19; William S. Smedlund, *Camp Fires of Georgia's Troops, 1861-1865* (Sharpsburg GA, 1994) 268; A. P. Adamson, *Brief History of the Thirtieth Georgia Regiment* (Griffin GA, 1912) 23-25; William Harris Bragg, "Joe Brown vs. the Confederacy," *Civil War Times Illustrated* 26 (November 1987): 39; Charles H. Calhoun, Sr., *Dr. Lindsey Durham: A Brief Biography; "The Durham Doctors: Biographical Sketches* (n.p., 1965) 43; National Archives Microfilm Publications, *Confederate Papers Relating to Citizens of Business Firms*, No. 346, Roll 383 (Washington, 1961) various locations; *Southern Recorder*, 14 April 1863; *Macon Telegraph*, 18 July 1864.

[22] Lillian Henderson, compiler, *Roster of the Confederate Soldiers of Georgia*, 6 vols. (Hapeville GA, 1959-1964) 6:789; Williams, *History of Jones County*, 642-43; Eliza Frances Andrews, "A Visit to Clinton," *Jones County News*, 18 April 1901.

[23] Samuel Griswold Johnson to Louisa Griswold, 12 May, 30 November 1861, United Daughters of the Confederacy, Georgia Division, Bound Typescripts (14 vols., GDAH) 4:379-82; S. H. Griswold, "Pine Ridge Church in the Long Ago," *Jones County News*, 22 October 1908; Lynn E. Wolff, *Old Clinton Cemetery* (n.p., 1978) 52.

[24] Hardeman Memoir; William A. Albaugh III et al., *Confederate Handguns* (Philadelphia, 1967) 24-25.

[25] Hardeman Memoir; George W. Gunnison, *A Genealogy of the Descendants of Hugh Gunnison* (Boston, 1880) 117; Ezra S. Stearns, compiler, *Genealogical and Family History of the State of New Hampshire* 4 vols. (New York, 1908) 4:1846; Albaugh et al., *Confederate Handguns*, 33-34; Samuel Griswold Letter, GDAH; New Orleans City Directories, 1857-1861; A. N. Gunnison to G. W. Randolph, 14 May 1862, in Wiley Sword, *Firepower from Abroad: The Confederate Enfield and the Le Mat Revolver, 1861-1863 with New Data on a Variety of Confederate Small Arms* (Lincoln RI, 1986) 110.

[26] William A. Albaugh III, *The Confederate Brass-Framed Colt and Whitney* (Falls Church VA, 1955) 8-11. These pistols are now, of course, worth considerably more than what Griswold & Gunnison were paid for them, with published estimates ranging from

$2500 for a poor specimen to $8500 for one in good condition (Ned Schwing, *1998 Standard Catalog of Firearms* [Iola, WI] 413), but prices now often begin in the $10,000–$15,000 range.

[27] *Macon Telegraph*, 5 August 1862.

[28] Albaugh et al., *Confederate Handguns*, 29, 32. This source (32) gives the following general specifications for the Griswold & Gunnison pistol—total length: c. 13 inches; barrel: iron, 7 1/2" (round; lands and grooves: 6, twisted right); barrel frame: brass, 1 15/16" inches long, round (earliest models) or partially octagonal; cylinder: iron, 1 3/4" (length), 1 9/16" (diameter); foresight, trigger guard, and backstrap: brass.

[29] Albaugh, *Confederate Colt*, 9; *Macon Telegraph*, 2 November 1863. In 1865 Griswold valued his slave "mechanics" at $5000 each (Depredation Affidavit).

[30] Adjutant General's Office, Letter Book B-44, 2 vols., 2:424, GDAH.

[31] Albaugh and Simmons, *Confederate Arms*, 241, 243; William Harris Bragg, "The Union General Lost in Georgia," 24 *Civil War Times Illustrated* (June 1985): 1920.

[32] Bragg, "Union General," 19-20; Shelby Foote, *The Civil War: A Narrative* 3 vols. (New York, 1958-1974) 3:318; Mary Callaway Jones, *Some Historic Spots of the Confederacy in Macon* (Macon GA, 1937) 1, 11-13.

[33] *Official Records*, 38 (Part 1):75-76; Albert Castel, *Decision in the West: The Atlanta Campaign of 1864* (Lawrence KS, 1992) 437-38, 569; David Evans, *Sherman's Horsemen: Union Cavalry Operations in the Atlanta Campaign* (Bloomington IN, 1996) 205-206.

[34] Morton R. McInvale, "'That Thing of Infamy,' Macon's Camp Oglethorpe during the Civil War," *Georgia Historical Quarterly* 63 (Summer 1979): 279, 284, 289; William Best Hesseltine, *Civil War Prisons* (Columbus OH, 1930) 161; Ovid L. Futch, *History of Andersonville Prison* (Gainesville FL, 1968) 31; William Marvel, *Andersonville: The Last Depot* (Chapel Hill, 1994) 284n.39; Bragg, "The Union General," 18.

[35] George W. Cullum, *Biographical Register of the Officers and Graduates of the US Military Academy* 2 vols. (Boston and New York, 1891) 2:280-81; Jacob Dolson Cox, *Military Reminiscences of the Civil War* 2 vols. (New York, 1900) 2:463; Stephen Z. Starr, *The Union Cavalry in the Civil War* 3 vols. (Baton Rouge LA, 1979-1985) 1:362, 368n.6, 2:5, 501; Bragg, "The Union General," 18.

[36] Sidney C. Kerksis, ed., *The Atlanta Papers* (Dayton OH, 1980) 668; Eastham Tarrant, *The Wild Riders of the First Kentucky Cavalry* (Louisville KY, 1894) 34; Bragg, "The Union General," 16.

[37] Starr, *Union Cavalry*, 3:465; Castel, *Decision in the West*, 17.

[38] Washington L. Sanford, *History of the Fourteenth Illinois Cavalry* (Chicago IL, 1898) 185-86; *Official Records*, 38, Part 1:76, Part 2,:763, 915, 919; Part 5,:409; *Atlanta Daily Intelligencer*, 4 August 1864; Tarrant, *Wild Riders*, 360, 369, 375; Evans, *Sherman's Horsemen*, 25.

[39] Williams, *History of Jones County*, 49.

[40] *Official Records*, 38, Part 2:920-26; Tarrant, *Wild Riders*, 361-62; *Columbus Daily Sun*, 20 August 1864.

[41] *Augusta Chronicle & Sentinel*, 5 August 1864; *Macon Telegraph*, 4 August 1864.

[42] Ibid.; Louise Caroline Reese Cornwell, "A Paper Written and read…in the late Sixties," *Confederate Diaries*, Vol. 5 (UDC, 1940) 249 (GDAH); *Augusta Chronicle & Sentinel*, 5 August 1864; Evans, *Sherman's Horsemen*, 295-96. The McKissick house still stood in 1999, just north of Hillsboro on State Highway 11, a two-story house distinguished by large chimneys.

[43] *Official Records*, 38, Part 2:926; *Official Records*, Part 5:251; *Reports of the Presidents and Superintendents of the Central Railroad and Banking Company of Georgia, from No. 20 to 32 Inclusive* (Savannah GA, 1868) 77.

[44] Horace Montgomery, *Howell Cobb's Confederate Career* (Tuscaloosa AL, 1959) 115; Ezra J. Warner, *Generals in Gray* (Baton Rouge LA, 1959) 55; Middle Georgia Historical Society, *Macon…An Architectural & Historical Guide* (Macon GA, 1996) 28-29.

[45] William Harris Bragg, *Joe Brown's Army* (Macon GA, 1987) viii-xi, 7-9; *Annual Report of the Adjutant and Inspector General of the State of Georgia* (Milledgeville, 1864) 4-6 & Table No. 1 (hereafter cited as *AIG's 1864 Report*); Montgomery, *Cobb's Career*, 115. The Confederate Reserve Force was conceived in Richmond with a two-fold purpose. The creation of the force was meant to allay the Confederate governors' legitimate concerns regarding local defense, while—it was forlornly hoped—weaning them away from their own solution to local defense: state armies, such as those created by Governor Brown and others (Albert Burton Moore, *Conscription and Conflict in the Confederacy* [New York, 1924] 308-311; *Official Records*, Series 4, 3:178-81).

[46] Parks, *Joseph E. Brown*, 282-88; Pleasant A. Stovall, *Robert Toombs* (New York, 1892) 278.

[47] Parks, *Joseph E. Brown*, 281, 289, 293; Evans, *Sherman's Horsemen*, 297-99.

[48] Arthur E. Boardman Letter, 28 April 1929, Genealogical & Historical Room, Washington Memorial Library, Macon GA; J. W. Mallet, "Memoranda of my life—for my children," Accession No. 20, University of Virginia Library, Charlottesville VA; Albaugh, *Confederate Colt*, 70.

[49] G. W. Lee, "Official Report of the Battle of East Macon, July 30, 1864," dated 4 August 1864 (hereafter cited as Lee's Report) Cobb Papers, Hargrett Library, University of Georgia Libraries, Athens GA (location hereafter cited as Hargrett Library); U. B. Phillips, ed., *The Correspondence of Robert Toombs, Alexander H. Stephens and Howell Cobb* (Washington, DC, 1913) 650; Broadside, "To the Citizens of Macon…," (Macon, Georgia, 1864), Hargrett Library.

[50] Lee's Report, Hargrett Library; *Atlanta Daily Intelligencer*, 3, 4 August 1864; *Christian Index*, 9, 12 August 1864.

[51] Ibid.

[52] John K. Mahon, *History of the Militia and the National Guard* (New York, 1983) 78-84. Longstreet's *Georgia Scenes* (Augusta GA, 1835) contained "The Militia Company Drill" (actually written by Oliver Hillhouse Prince), and Thompson's "The Militia Muster" appeared in his *Major Jones's Courtship* (Philadelphia, 1840). The "Bill Arp"

columns on the Georgia Militia in the Civil War were included in the collection *Bill Arp, So Called* (New York, 1866).

[53] James Horace Bass, "Georgia in the Confederacy, 1861-1865" (Ph.D. diss., University of Texas, 1932) 90-92; Wilbur G. Kurtz, "Whitehall Tavern," *The Atlanta Historical Bulletin* (April 1931): 46; Lyle D. Brundage, "The Organization, Administration, and Training of the United States Ordinary and Volunteer Militia, 1792-1861" (Ed.D diss., University of Michigan, 1958) 16-18; *Governor Brown's Proclamations and Orders Calling into Active Military Service and Sending to the Front the Civil and Military Officers, and the Reserved Militia of the State of Georgia, to the Army of Tennessee* (Milledgeville GA, 1864) 3; Joseph E. Johnston, *Narrative of Military Operations* (New York, 1874) 369-70; S. H. Griswold, "Stoneman's Raid," *Jones County News*, 4 March 1909.

[54] *Official Records*, 38, Part 2:926; Kerksis, *Atlanta Papers*, 677; *Confederate Union*, 9 August 1864.

[55] Mary A. H. Gay, *Life in Dixie during the War* (Atlanta GA, 1897) 196; *Macon Telegraph*, 26 August 1864.

[56] *Columbus Daily Sun*, 2 August 1864; Receipt, 31 August 1864, National Archives, *Confederate Papers*.

[57] *Official Records*, 38, Part 2:916; *Christian Index*, 12 August 1864; Lee's Report, Hargrett Library; Griswold, "Stoneman's Raid."

[58] Robert H. Kingman, Sr., Deposition, *Reminiscences of Confederate Soldiers*, Vol. XII (UDC, 1940) 248; *Macon Telegraph*, 23 September 1934.

[59] Griswold, "Stoneman's Raid."

[60] James Cooper Nisbet, *Four Years on the Firing Line*, edited by Bell I. Wiley (Jackson TN, 1963) 245-46.

[61] *Official Records*, 38, Part 2:916; *Columbus Daily Sun*, 2, 3 August 1864; John C. Butler, *Historical Record of Macon and Central Georgia* (Macon GA, 1879) 264; *Macon Telegraph*, 26 May 1907; "Map of the City of Macon, Ga.," RG 77:N 76-3, National Archives.

[62] *Official Records*, 38, Part 2:916; Lee's Report, Hargrett Library; *Christian Index*, 12 August 1864; *Columbus Daily Sun*, 3 August 1864; Asa B. Isham et al., *Prisoners of War and Military Prisons* (Cincinnati OH, 1890) 60; Joseph Ferguson, *Life-Struggles in Rebel Prisons* (Philadelphia PA, 1866) 113, 114.

[63] *Official Records*, 38, Part 2:916; Mary Ann Cobb to Mrs. Howell Cobb, 31 July 1864, Cobb Papers, Hargrett Library; Howell Cobb to his wife, 3 August 1864, Cobb Papers; *Macon Telegraph*, 2 August 1864; Johnston, *Narrative*, 370. For a more detailed account of the Battle of East Macon, see Evans, *Sherman's Horsemen*, 309-319.

[64] *Official Records*, 38, Part 2:916, 920.

[65] Kerksis, *Atlanta Papers*, 678; Sanford, *Fourteenth Illinois Cavalry*, 190-91.

[66] *Official Records*, 38, Part 3:680, 953, 957; W. C. Dodson, ed., *Campaigns of Wheeler and His Cavalry* (Atlanta GA, 1899) 233; Bennett H. Young, *Confederate Wizards of the Saddle* (Boston MA, 1914) 580; Williams, *History of Jones County*, 115.

[67] James M. Wells, *"With Touch of Elbow"* (Philadelphia PA, 1909) 211; *Official Records*, 38, Part 2:916; Kerksis, *Atlanta Papers*, 714.

[68] Sanford, *Fourteenth Illinois Cavalry*, 192; Tarrant, *Wild Riders*, 363; *Official Records*, 38, Part 2:916; *Augusta Chronicle & Sentinel*, 5 August 1864.

[69] Wells, *"With Touch of Elbow,"* 212-13; Tarrant, *Wild Riders*, 363; Bragg, "The Union General," 21; *Atlanta Daily Intelligencer*, 21 August 1864.

[70] John Robertson, compiler, *Michigan in the War* (Lansing MI, 1882) 697; Antonia Fraser, *Cromwell, the Lord Protector* (New York, 1973) 109.

[71] Kerksis, *Atlanta Papers*, 678; Sanford, *Fourteenth Illinois Cavalry*, 192-94, 296; *Official Records*, 38, Part 2:916, 927, 951-53, Part 4:791; Tarrant, *Wild Riders*, 369; *Atlanta Daily Intelligencer*, 21 August 1864; J. A. Wynn, "Memoir," in *Confederate Diaries* Vol. 5 (UDC, 1940) 58; O. P. Hargis, *Thrilling Experiences of a First Georgia Cavalryman in the Civil War* (Rome GA, n.d.) 22; Dodson, *Campaigns of Wheeler*, 232.

[72] Tarrant, *Wild Riders*, 364; W. C. Dodson, "Stampede of Federal Cavalry," *Confederate Veteran* 19 (March 1911): 124.

[73] *Official Records*, 38, Part 2:917, 920; Tarrant, *Wild Riders*, 364-66.

[74] Tarrant, *Wild Riders*, 364.

[75] Ibid., 369; Sanford, *Fourteenth Illinois Cavalry*, 199; David P. Conyngham, *Sherman's March Through the South* (New York, 1865) 186.

[76] *Atlanta Papers*, 683-84; Dodson, "Stampede," 123-24.

[77] Tarrant, *Wild Riders*, 367-68; Sanford, *Fourteenth Illinois Cavalry*, 203, 306; *Atlanta Papers*, 720.

[78] Wynn, "Memoir," 58-59.

[79] Cornwell, "A Paper," 251; *Official Records*, 38, Part 2:914; Wilbur F. Hinman, *The Story of the Sherman Brigade* (Alliance OH, 1897) 892; George Stoneman to his wife (telegram) 1 August 1864, William T. Sherman Papers, vol. 14, p.1882, Library of Congress; Wynn, "Memoir," 59; Hargis, *Thrilling Experiences*, 22; Conyngham, *Sherman's March*, 187; *ACS*, 5 August 1864; Young, *Confederate Wizards*, 594; Welsh, 323. Unlike Stoneman, Colonel Biddle was—under the circumstances—glad to see Colonel Crews, whom he knew as "a gallant officer, whose command I had often had skirmishes with, and with whom I had become acquainted. He took me in charge and I stayed with him that night, and he asked [General] Iverson to allow me to ride into Macon with him, the following morning, where I was to be put into the officers' prison." Biddle's brief account of the raid and its aftermath is included in Ellen McGowan Biddle, *Reminiscences of a Soldier's Life* (Philadelphia PA, 1907) 247-48.

[80] *Official Records*, 38, Part 5:937, Part 2:914; *New York Times*, 23 August 1864; *Columbus Daily Sun*, 4 August 1864; *Augusta Chronicle & Sentinel*, 5 August 1864; *Macon Telegraph*, 3 August 1864; Williams, *History of Jones County*, 147.

[81] Williams, *History of Jones County*, 149-53, 428. Much documentation of the story of Betty Hunt is in the Hunt Family Collection in the Middle Georgia Archives, Washington Memorial Library, Macon, Georgia, the gift of Dossie Hunt Teague, Mrs. Hunt's granddaughter

[82] *Atlanta Daily Intelligencer*, 4, 21 August 1864. The White house, no longer extant, was located just under four miles north of Stoneman's Hill, to the left of the Hillsboro road. The site is marked by the granite-walled family cemetery, and a photograph of the structure, far advanced into disrepair, is found in Williams, *History of Jones County*, 219. Another house on the White plantation (a slave dwelling some two miles from the battlefield—just within the maximum range of a Rodman gun) was struck by a Federal shell during the battle. Like those fired at Macon, the projectile did not explode (Williams, 272-73). This house was later incorporated into a larger residence, all but ruined by 1999, but still standing to the south of the Juliette Road, near its junction with State Highway 11.

[83] *Macon Telegraph*, 2, 3 August 1864; Dorence Atwater, *A List of the Union Soldiers Buried at Andersonville* (New York, 1866) various locations. Marvel in *Andersonville* (161) notes that at Andersonville's Camp Sumter in early August, during a "terrific thunderstorm," hundreds of captured Union troopers "trudged into the palisade," bringing the news of their and Stoneman's capture.

[84] *Macon Telegraph*, 4 August 1864; Wynn, "Memoir," 59. For Stoneman's Raid see also Evans, *Stoneman's Horsemen*, 291-376; William R. Scaife, *The Campaign for Atlanta* (Saline MI, 1985) 77-100; and Bragg, "The Union General," 16-23.

[85] Ezra J. Warner, *Generals in Blue* (Baton Rouge LA, 1964) 482; Castel, *Decision in the West*, 509, 548; Samuel Griswold to Col. James H. Burton, 28 October 1864, National Archives, *Confederate Papers*, various locations.

[86] Parks, *Joseph E. Brown*, 294-95; Charles C. Jones, Jr., *The Siege of Savannah in December 1864* (Albany NY) 3; Bragg, "Joe Brown vs. the Confederacy," 40; *AIG's 1864 Report*, 5. In September 1864, Major General G. W. Smith, commander of the First Division, Georgia Militia, claimed that during the Atlanta Campaign his force never exceeded 5000 men (*Official Records*, 38, Part 3:971). On 26 October 1864, however, Adjutant General Henry C. Wayne reported that during the campaign "between ten thousand and eleven thousand [militia] were armed, and put into the field" (*AIG's 1864 Report*, 5). See also Allen D. Candler, ed., *Confederate Records of the State of Georgia*, 5 vols. (Atlanta GA, 1909-1911) 2:774.

[87] *Macon Telegraph*, 17 November 1864; Robert Underwood Johnson and Clarence Clough Buel, eds., *Battles and Leaders of the Civil War* 4 vols.(New York, 1887-1888) 4:664. In allowing Hood's march into Tennessee, General P. G. T. Beauregard had persuaded himself that a force of about 30,000 men could be gathered in Georgia to confront Sherman's army, estimated by Beauregard at only 36,000 strong (*Official Records*, 44:932-33).

[88] William T. Sherman, *Memoirs of Gen. W. T. Sherman* 2 vols. (New York, 1891) 2:177. For the Battle of Griswoldville see William Harris Bragg, "A Little Battle at Griswoldville" *Civil War Times Illustrated* 19 (November 1980): 44-49, and Morton R. McInvale, "'All That Devils Could Wish For': The Griswoldville Campaign," *Georgia*

*Historical Quarterly* 60 (Summer 1976): 117-30. For the March to the Sea in general see Jones's *Siege of Savannah* (Albany, NY, 1874) Jacob D. Cox's *The March to the Sea—Franklin and Nashville* (New York, 1882), Burke Davis's *Sherman's March* (New York, 1980), and William R. Scaife's *The March to the Sea* (Saline MI, 1993) as well as the December 1989 issue of *Blue and Gray Magazine*, with Scaife's "Sherman's March to the Sea," illustrated with maps, archival photographs, and modern color views of several sites.

[89] Sherman, *Memoirs*, 2:173, 178-79. Savannah's population in 1860 was 22,292, comprising 13,875 whites and 8,417 slaves and free blacks (Alexander A. Lawrence, *A Present for Mr. Lincoln* [Macon GA, 1961] 4).

[90] *Official Records*, 44:411; Jones, *Siege of Savannah*, 3, 7, 89-91; Statistical Reports of the First Division, Georgia Militia, 31 October and 10 November 1864, GDAH. Only around 10,000 infantry and artillerymen could be assembled at Savannah to resist Sherman, and this number, plus Wheeler's 3500 troopers, is probably the best estimate of Hardee's force in Georgia during the March to the Sea, though there were garrison forces elsewhere, particularly at Augusta, long presumed to be Sherman's target (B. H. Liddell Hart, *Sherman: Soldier, Realist, American* [New York, 1929] 338, 341). For various (and often contradictory) number estimates of the forces available to the Confederacy in Georgia during Sherman's March, see *Official Records*, 44:883-84, 896, 901, 905, 908, 921, 932-33, 959, 965, 974, and 1000.

[91] *Official Records*, 44:411-12; Dodson, *Campaigns of Wheeler*, 404-405, 420. The newspapers of the time, as well as Governor Brown's incoming correspondence, contain numerous complaints regarding the depredations of Wheeler's cavalry (or, mounted bands assumed to be Wheeler's cavalry). The two sources cited above attempt to absolve Wheeler's men of most of the charges. Governor Brown was unconvinced, however, and his papers in Special Collections, Duke University Library, contain numerous documented charges, including a claim by the governor himself that he had witnessed looting by officers and men of Wheeler's command in Atlanta in July 1864 (Brown to P. G. T. Beauregard, 8 April 1865, Joseph E. Brown Papers, Special Collections, Duke University Library, Durham, North Carolina [hereafter cited as Duke]).

[92] Sam R. Watkins, *"Co. Aytch"* (Chattanooga TN, 1900) 175; Bragg, "Little Battle," 45; Louise Biles Hill, *Joseph E. Brown and the Confederacy* (Chapel Hill NC, 1939) 83, 124; Bragg, *Joe Brown's Army*, ix-xi.

[93] Howell Cobb to Charles C. Jones, Jr., [c. September 1867], Charles C. Jones, Jr., Papers, Duke; William Harris Bragg, "Howell Cobb's Account," *Civil War Times Illustrated* 20 (August 1981): 30-31.

[94] Liddell Hart, *Sherman*, 331-32, 336-38.

[95] *Official Records*, 44:8; Sherman, *Memoirs*, 2:175, 178.

[96] Warner, *Generals in Blue*, 266-67; James Harrison Wilson, *Under the Old Flag*, 2 vols. (New York, 1912) 2:13.

[97] *Official Records*, 44:54, 362; Ruby Felder Ray, ed., *Letters and Diary of Lieut. Lavender R. Ray, 1861-1865* (n. p., 1949) 14.

[98] *Official Records*, 44:861, 862, 865; Jones, *Siege of Savannah*, 15-17; Albaugh, *Confederate Colt*, 75-76.

[99] *Official Records*, 44:865, 869. Judging by a comment he made to Mrs. Braxton Bragg, General Lee—like General Beauregard—overestimated the Southern forces available to oppose Sherman's March, and underestimated Sherman's numbers, remarking that "if the Georgians are true to themselves Sherman can't escape" (Judith Lee Hallock, "Braxton Bragg and Confederate Defeat" [Ph.D. diss., State University of New York at Stony Brook, 1989] 341).

[100] Ray, ed., *Letters and Diary*, 15; *Macon Telegraph*, 18, 21 November 1864; *Columbus Daily Sun*, 29 November 1864; *Official Records*, 44:66, 369, 868; Cox, *Military Reminisces*, 26-27.

[101] *Official Records*, 44:66; *Ninety-second Illinois Volunteers* (Freeport IL, 1875) 175-76.

[102] Cornelius C. Platter, Civil War Diary, 1864-1865 (Manuscript) 20 November 1864, Hargrett Library (hereafter cited as Platter Diary).

[103] *Official Records*, 44:8-9.

[104] Ibid., 81-82.

[105] *Ninety-second Illinois*, 176.

[106] Richard Henry Hutchings, *Hutchings, Bonner, Wyatt: An Intimate Family History* (Utica NY, 1937) 146; *Official Records*, 44:54, 82.

[107] George W. Pepper, *Personal Recollections of Sherman's Campaigns in Georgia and the Carolinas* (Zanesvile OH, 1866) 241.

[108] Platter Diary, 23 November 1864; *Macon Telegraph*, 29 November 1864.

[109] *Macon Telegraph*, 29 November 1864.

[110] S.H. Griswold, "A Little War History," *Jones County News*, 7 May 1908.

[111] *Macon Telegraph*, 29 November 1864.

[112] Platter Diary, 21 November 1864; Pepper, *Personal Recollections*, 241.

[113] *Official Records*, 44:406, 414, 417; Dodson, *Campaigns of Wheeler*, 287.

[114] *Official Records*, 44:406-407. In late November, Wheeler still estimated Sherman's force at half its actual strength (*Official Records*, 44:901).

[115] *Official Records*, 44:407.

[116] *Official Records*, 44:390; James Moore, *Kilpatrick and Our Cavalry* (New York, 1865) 178; *Macon Telegraph*, 30 November 1864.

[117] *Macon Telegraph*, 30 November 1864.

[118] *Official Records*, 44:390, 396; Isaac W. Avery, *History of the State Of Georgia* (New York, 1881) 311.

[119] *Official Records*, 53:32; *Official Records*, 44:390, 396, 886.

[120] Jane McIntosh Wagener, "General Kilpatrick's Cavalry in Sherman's March to the Sea" (M.A. thesis, University of Georgia, 1957) 58.

[121] Frank Moore, ed., *The Rebellion Record* 11 vols. (New York, 1861-1868) 9:163, 171; *Official Records*, 44:886.

[122] *Official Records*, 44:414, 886; *Macon Telegraph*, 30 November 1864; Hardee to Beauregard, 21 November 1864 (two telegrams) P. G. T. Beauregard Papers, Duke.

[123] *Official Records*, 44:369, 379, 407, 509, 511-12; S. H. Griswold, "The Cotton Gin"; *Macon Telegraph*, 23 November 1864; *Columbus Daily Sun*, 25 November 1864; Ray, ed., *Letters and Diary*, 16.

[124] *Official Records*, 44:508-509; Oliver Otis Howard, *Autobiography of Oliver Otis Howard, Major General, United States Army*, 2 vols. (New York, 1907) 2:71; Warner, *Generals in Blue*, 237-38; Henry H. Wright, *A History of the Sixth Iowa Infantry* (Iowa City IA, 1923) 362-63; Bragg, "A Little Battle," 45; Platter Diary, 22 November 1864; *Official Records*, 44:93-94, 405.

[125] *Official Records*, 44:508; Howard, *Autobiography*, 2:71; Wright, *History of the Sixth Iowa*, 362-63.

[126] *Official Records*, 44:66, 82, 509; W. B. Hazen, *A Narrative of Military Service* (Boston MA, 1885) 315.

[127] *Official Records*, 44:82, 509, 510; Howard, *Autobiography*, 2:71, 74.

[128] *Official Records*, 44:886; Hardee to Beauregard, 21 November 1864 (two telegrams) Beauregard Papers, Duke; *Lloyd's Southern Railroad Guide* (Atlanta GA, [1864]) various locations; *Official Records*, 44:414-15, 877.

[129] *Official Records*, 44:369, 379, 382, 387, 407. 509, 511-12, 880; Ray, ed., *Letters and Diary*, 16.

[130] *Official Records*, 44:886, 369, 382, 386-87; S. H. Griswold, "Courage and Patriotism of Our Ancestors," *Jones County News*, 18 March 1909. The Griswold article cited describes an encounter at the Griswold house between General Wheeler and one of Samuel Griswold's grandsons, then very young, who "like a small boy would worm around the officers" and try to take their measure. He assumed that Wheeler, "very young and small" himself, was a "3rd Lieutenant," much to the general's amusement.

[131] *Official Records*, 44:369, 382, 386-87. The Ninth Pennsylvania Cavalry was the main Union force involved in this skirmish.

[132] *Official Records*, 44:105; Michael Fellman, *Citizen Sherman* (New York, 1995) 140. Fellman's book offers an unsparing and persuasive assessment of Sherman's character in general and his actions during the March to the Sea in particular.

[133] Wright, *History of the Sixth Iowa*, 365; *Official Records*, 44:82-83, 382, 387, 407.

[134] *Official Records*, 44:82-83.

[135] Deed Book R, 314; *Official Records*, 44:83; S. H. Griswold, "Unwritten History. A Battle Fought in Jones County but Never Recorded," *Jones County News*, 3 July 1908; Cox, *Military Reminiscences*, 2:30. Cox's *The March to the Sea—Franklin and Nashville* (New York, 1882) offers a useful survey of Sherman's March.

[136] Griswold, "Unwritten History"; Milledgeville *Federal Union*, 7 October 1856; Interview with Charles F. Wells, 5 November 1977, in private possession. Elder Wells

(1905-1990) was pastor of Mountain Springs Church from 1936 and for many years lived on the site of the Griswold & Gunnison pistol factory. His lifelong study of Griswoldville and the military operations in its vicinity culminated in his booklet *The Battle of Griswoldville: 'Georgia's Gettysburg,' November 21-22, 1864* (Macon GA, 1961), which contains much lore not found elsewhere, often drawn from oral traditions.

[137] *Official Records*, 44:97-98; Wright, *History of the Sixth Iowa*, 366; *Official Records*, 53:44; Griswold, "Unwritten History"; *Reminiscences of the Civil War from Diaries of Members of the 103d Illinois Volunteer Infantry* (Chicago IL, 1904) 154.

[138] Wright, *History of the Sixth Iowa*, 366; Charles W. Wills, *Army Life of an Illinois Soldier* (Washington, DC, 1906) 323.

[139] *Official Records*, 44:382, 407.

[140] *Official Records*, 44:414; Douglas Southall Freeman, *Lee's Lieutenants*, 3 vols. (New York, 1942-1944) 1:262n.99; Henderson, *Roster*, 3:576; Adjutant General's Office, Book of Commissions, Vol. B-49, 1861-1865, various locations, GDAH; John H. Martin, *Columbus, Georgia: 1827-1865* 2 vols. (Columbus GA, 1874-1875) 2: 159; P. J. Philips Correspondence File, GDAH; *Columbus Daily Enquirer-Sun*, 13 October 1876. G. W. Smith's wartime and post-bellum accounts of military operations often contradict each other. In the text, Smith's after-action reports and other sources have been given precedence over his two brief memoirs, published in *Battles and Leaders of the Civil War*, when there are discrepancies.

[141] Bragg, *Joe Brown's Army*, viii, 36-38, 87.

[142] Joseph T. Derry, *Georgia*, vol. 6 of *Confederate Military History*, 12 vols. (Atlanta GA, 1899) 471; Biographical Sketch of Henry Greaves, in private possession; G. W. Smith, "The Georgia Militia about Atlanta," in Johnson and Buel, eds., *Battles and Leaders*, 4:332.

[143] *Official Records*, 53:41; Jack H. King, Georgia Militia, to his wife, 23 November 1864, Civil War Miscellany, GDAH; *Columbus Daily Sun*, 26 November 1864; Davis, *Sherman's March*, 143; Mary G. Jones and Lily Reynolds, eds., *Coweta County Chronicles* (Atlanta GA, 1928) 154; Griswold, "Unwritten History." No precise numbers have been found for the forces thrown against the Federals at Griswoldville; those mentioned in the text are based upon the Tri-Monthly Report of the First Division, Georgia Militia, 10 November 1864, GDAH; G. W. Smith to Richard Taylor, 19 November 1864 (*Official Records*, 44:417-18); G. W. Smith to Hardee, 6 December 1864 (*Official Records*, 44:413-17, & G. W. Smith Papers, Duke); Rations Statement, Savannah Garrison, 16 December 1864 (Charles C. Jones, Jr., *The Siege of Savannah in December, 1864* [Albany NY, 1874] 89-91); George T. Jackson to Charles C. Jones, Jr., undated, Charles C. Jones, Jr., Papers, Duke; and G. W. Smith, "The Georgia Militia during Sherman's March to the Sea," in Johnson and Buel, eds., *Battles and Leaders*, 4:667. Though data from G. W. Smith must be used with caution, other documentation supports his suggestion that the Confederate forces at Griswoldville numbered fewer than 2400 (*Official Records*, 44:414) with around 2300—including the militiamen, State Line, Confederate Reserves, and Confederate artillery—probably a good estimate.

[144] *Official Records*, 53:41; *Southern Watchman* (Athens GA) 12 November 1862; Charles J. Brockman, Jr., "Life in Confederate Athens, Georgia," *Georgia Review* 21 (Spring 1967): 117; Charles J. Brockman, Jr., "The Confederate Armory of Cook and Brother," in *Papers of the Athens Historical Society* 2 (1979) 76-79; Albaugh and Simmons, *Confederate Arms*, 212; George T. Jackson to Charles C. Jones, Jr., undated, Charles C. Jones, Jr., Papers, Duke; *Columbus Daily Sun*, 26 November 1864. The number of reserves is an estimate based on Jackson's letter, various Griswoldville and Honey Hill casualty lists published in contemporary newspapers, and information from *Compiled Service Records of Confederate Soldiers Who Served in Organizations from the State of Georgia*, National Archives Microfilm Publication Microcopy No. 266, Rolls 126, 127, and 128 (Colonel George W. Rains's First Regiment, Local Defense Troops, Augusta, Georgia).

[145] *Reports of the Operations of the Militia, from October 13, 1864, to February 11, 1865, by Maj.-Generals G. W. Smith and Wayne, together with Memoranda by Gen. Smith, for the Improvement of the State Military Organization* (Macon GA, 1865) 12-13; Richard Taylor, *Destruction and Reconstruction* (New York, 1879) 212.

[146] *Official Records*, 53:41; A. J. Jackson, "Diary of the War Between the States kept by A. J. Jackson, Company G, Georgia State Line Troops, from February, 1863, to April, 1865 [Manuscript]," Microfilm Box 76-7, pages 6-7, GDAH.

[147] *Official Records*, 53:40-41.

[148] *Official Records*, 53:40-43; Griswold, "Unwritten History"; Scaife, *March to the Sea*, 37; Robertson, *Michigan in the War*, 523 (This source prints Union artillerist A. F. R. Arndt's after-action report, dated 27 November 1864, not found in the *Official Records*). The Pennsylvania-born General McCay's name "was pronounced as though it were spelled McCoy," as it is sometimes misspelled (Alexander A. Lawrence, "Henry Kent McCay—Forgotten Jurist" 9 *Georgia Bar Journal* [August 1946]: 5).

Even after Smith decided to extricate Philips's force, the orders he sent specified mainly that Philips was to "avoid a fight with a superior force" and that if "pressed by a superior force fall back…without bringing on a serious engagement if you can do so." In his report to General Hardee of 6 December 1864 (written, incidentally, before receiving the after-action reports of Philips and other participants on 25 January 1865), Smith asserted that his orders to Philips directed him "to avoid an engagement at that place and time"—a statement not supported by the other documentation. Philips did not record in his official report what his orders had been. The available information, ambiguous as it is, makes it difficult to argue that Philips disobeyed orders in attacking (*Reports of the Operations*, 3, 5, 12-13, 15).

[149] Wright, *History of the Sixth Iowa*, 366-67; A. F. R. Arndt, *Reminiscences of an Artillery Officer* (Detroit MI, 1890) 8; Robertson, *Michigan in the War*, 23.

[150] *Reminiscences of the 103d Illinois*, 154-55; Wright, *History of the Sixth Iowa*, 366-67; *Official Records*, 53:28, 42.

[151] *Official Records*, 53:43-44.

[152] *Official Records*, 53:43-44; Griswold, "Unwritten History"; Wills, *Army Life*, 324; *Official Records*, 53:29; *Reminiscences of the 103d Illinois*, 155.

[153] *Official Records*, 44:97; Wright, *History of the Sixth Iowa*, 367. Though Evans does not mention the number of charges made from the streambed, Federal reports most often mention three, with some counting as many as seven.

[154] Dallas D. Irvine, *Military Operations of the Civil War, A Guide-Index to the Official Records* 5 vols. (Washington, DC, 1966-1980/US National Archives Microfilm M1036) 1:1394; *Grier's Southern Almanac* (Augusta GA, 1864) 17; Jackson, "Diary," 7; Felix Pryor to wife, 23 November 1864, in Mills Lane, ed., *"Dear Mother: Don't grieve about me. If I get killed, I'll only be dead": Letters from Georgia Soldiers in the Civil War* (Savannah GA, 1977) 336; *Macon Telegraph*, 23-24 November 1864; "Beverly Daniel Evans," Book of Minutes 'H,' Folio 170, Washington County Courthouse, Sandersville GA; Lane, ed., *"Dear Mother,"* 335.

[155] *Official Records*, 53:40-43; *Columbus Daily Sun*, 25 November 1864. Some of the wounded militiamen were also sent as far south as Americus, where they were the subject of jokes from the Confederates in the hospital there, but received some credit as well. "One poor boy," wrote Confederate nurse Kate Cumming, "said the battle was the most *terrible* of the war. It was quite a severe fight. The enemy set a trap, and the unsophisticated militia were caught in it. I believe there were at least one hundred killed and many wounded, and I am told they were nearly all old men. The *veterans* whom I have heard speak of the fight say that old soldiers would never have rushed in as the militia did." But, she continued, "Joe Brown's Pets' have done much better than anyone expected; they have fought well when they have had it to do" (Richard Barksdale Harwell, ed., *Kate: The Journal of a Confederate Nurse* [Baton Rouge LA, 1959] 241).

[156] Welsh, 356-57; Wright, *History of the Sixth Iowa*, 367-68.

[157] *Official Records*, 44:105, 53:42; Derry, *Georgia*, 470; *Macon Telegraph*, 24 November 1864.

[158] George Ward Nichols, *The Story of the Great March* (New York, 1865) 64; Eli J. Sherlock, *Memorabilia of the Marches and Battles in Which the One Hundredth Regiment of Indiana Volunteers Took an Active Part* (Kansas City MO, 1896) 163; Wright, *History of the Sixth Iowa*, 363; Wills, *Army Life*, 324; Theodore F. Upson, *With Sherman to the Sea* (Baton Rouge LA, 1943) 138. Confederate soldiers in the past had also found themselves sadly affected by the deaths of those they had ridiculed. Sam Watkins' amusing description of the militia at Atlanta is often quoted, but the end of his passage is not. It describes one of the skirmishes participated in by "Joe Brown's Pets," and the bringing back to camp of their casualties: "these dead and wounded men…made a more serious impression on my mind than in any previous or subsequent battles," he recalled (Watkins, *"Co. Aytch,"* 176).

159 *Official Records*, 53:39; Wills, *Army Life*, 324; Andrew Bush to Mary Bush, 20 December 1864, Andrew Bush File, Indiana State Library, Indianapolis, IN; *Macon Telegraph*, 24 November 1864; *Columbus Daily Sun*, 29 November 1864. General Smith's first report stated casualties of "a little over six hundred," later corrected to "51 killed and 472 wounded" (*Report of the Operations*, 5, 15).

[160] Upson, *With Sherman to the Sea*, 138; Wright, *History of the Sixth Iowa*, 367, 369, 371.

[161] Jones, *Siege of Savannah*, 90; *Reports of the Operations*, 5, 23-24. Philips was not permanently relieved from duty. He was, in fact, back in command of his brigade by January 1865 (*Official Records*, 47, Part 2:1071). This reference is among the many that sow confusion about the nature of Georgia troops; it lists Philips's command as the "Second Brigade Georgia Reserves." Though the men were in the militia reserve (as opposed to the militia proper) the troops more usually known as reserves during the war's last year belonged to Howell Cobb's Confederate Reserve Force.

[162] Griswold, "Unwritten History"; S. H. Griswold, "Passing of Stoneman's and Sherman's Armies," *Jones County News*, 19 November 1908; Bragg, "A Little Battle," 49; Wright, *History of the Sixth Iowa*, 368.

[163] Bragg, "A Little Battle," 45; Patricia L. Faust, ed., *Historical Times Illustrated Encyclopedia of the Civil War* (New York, 1986) 305; Richard Barksdale Harwell, ed., *Songs of the Confederacy* (New York, 1951) 100-101; *Official Records*, Series 4, 3:48.

[164] *Macon Telegraph*, 24 November 1864; Conyngham, *Sherman's March*, 68.

[165] Nichols, *Story of the Great March*, 64; Wills, *Army Life*, 324; Henry Hitchcock, *Marching with Sherman* (New Haven, 1927) 168; Upson, *With Sherman to the Sea*, 138.

[166] Jones, *Siege of Savannah*, 27. In later years, the importance of the battle was inflated, contrary to fact, by such writers as Augustus Longstreet Hull, who asserted that the battle "saved Macon from the fate of Atlanta" (A. L. Hull, *The Campaigns of the Confederate Army* [Atlanta, 1901] 80). Governor Brown himself, however, had made the same argument in January 1865: without the protection of Georgia state troops, Brown wrote Secretary of War James Seddon, "Macon must have shared the fate of Atlanta...." (Candler, ed., *Confederate Records*, 3:688-89).

[167] *Official Records*, 44:83; Stephen Graham, "Marching Through Georgia," *Harper's Monthly Magazine* 140 (April 1920): 615. In Clinton, the courthouse had been extensively vandalized, as attested to in January 1875 by Roland T. Ross, county ordinary. In one of the damaged county record books he wrote, "This Record was wantonly defaced and mutilated by the Yankee Army under Genl Sherman in his march through Georgia 1864, and many other records were torn out and destroyed without any cause or benefit to the Army—save that low desire to injure and oppress a people because their only crime was to live in a Southern clime & defend their own rights." (County Affairs, 1842-1888, Probate Court, p. 307, Jones County Courthouse).

[168] Warner, *Generals in Blue*, 535; Sherman, *Memoirs*, 2:188; Jones, *Siege of Savannah*, 77; *Official Records*, 44:585-86.

[169] *Official Records*, 44:414-15. Because of the Federal activities in the Griswoldville area, Carswell's First Brigade, Georgia Militia, apparently retired south down the Marion Road (as Philips was later advised to do, and as Wheeler did) and returned to Macon by a circuitous route. In any case, the brigade had not returned to Macon by 11:00 PM on 23 November, when Wheeler was queried regarding the missing militiamen's whereabouts (*Official Records*, 44:888-89). Some Federal accounts of the cavalry skirmish on the morning of the 22nd, and its aftermath, mention Rebel infantry, suggesting possible involvement by Carswell's militiamen in the fighting (*Official Records*, 53:39; *Official Records*, 44:382).

[170] Smith, "The Georgia Militia during Sherman's March to the Sea," in Johnson and Buel, eds., *Battles and Leaders*, 4:668; *Official Records*, 44:415-16, 906, 914; Luis F. Emilio, *History of the Fifty-fourth Regiment of Massachusetts Volunteer Infantry* (Boston MA, 1894) 241-51; Jones, *Siege of Savannah*, 91; Foote, *The Civil War*, 3:652-53; William Harris Bragg, "The Fight at Honey Hill," 22 *Civil War Times Illustrated* (January 1984): 18-19. Elsewhere, General Hardee lists his effectives evacuated from Savannah at 7300 men (Hardee to Charles C. Jones, Jr., 14 May 1866, Georgia Portfolio II, Charles C. Jones, Jr., Papers, Duke). General Smith's eagerness to have Colcock command at Honey Hill, like his absence from Griswoldville, suggests much, as does the fact that Smith gave Colcock no credit in the account of the battle he wrote for *Battles and Leaders* (4:668-69). Colcock's own description of the battle is found in a letter to his cousin, Charles Colcock Jones, Jr. (5 November 1867, Charles C. Jones, Jr., Papers, Duke) and is used in a lengthier account, "The Battle of Honey Hill" by Charles J. Colcock, Jr., Colonel Colcock's son, in the Charleston SC, *Sunday News*, 10 December 1899.

[171] Bragg, *Joe Brown's Army*, 105-111; James Pickett Jones, *Yankee Blitzkrieg* (Athens GA, 1976) xi, 166-67, 178; McInvale, "'That Thing of Infamy,'" 289; G. W. Smith to C. C. Jones, Jr., 3 October 1867, Charles C. Jones, Jr., Papers, Duke. According to Butler's *History of Macon* (286), "On the night of the 22d [of April 1865], the [Union] soldiers set fire to two blocks on [Macon's] Mulberry street, and a portion of buildings on each, comprising valuable property, was destroyed." This account tallies with Smith's statement, cited in the letter above, that the "records of the Militia of Georgia were destroyed by the burning of the building in which they were contained, some two days after the occupation of Macon" on 20 April.

[172] Pratt, *Daniel Pratt*, 17, 20; *Historical Guide*, 2; Griswold, "The Cotton Gin;" Albaugh, *Confederate Colt*, 17; William A. Gary, *Confederate Revolvers* (Dallas TX, 1987) 8. See also National Archives Microfilm Publications, *Records of Ordnance Establishments at Macon, Georgia*, No. NNO781, Reel 9, Washington, DC, 1971), various locations.

[173] Deed Book S, 480; Deed Book T, 83; and Deed Book S, 502; (Macon) *Georgia Journal and Messenger*, 2 October 1867; Wolff, *Old Clinton Cemetery*, 51.

[174] Allen D. Candler and Clement A. Evans, eds., *Georgia*, 3 vols. (Atlanta GA, 1906) 2:169; Williams, *History of Jones County*, 296; Deed Book 3J, 454; Richard J. Lenz, *The Civil War in Georgia: An Illustrated Traveler's Guide* (Watkinsville GA, 1995) 82. Lenz's book contains information on many Middle Georgia sites relating to the Atlanta and Savannah Campaigns, including directions to most sites. The author's "Do's and Don'ts" (3) should be scrupulously heeded, particularly his warning against trespassing on private property.

In the summer of 1997, the Georgia Civil War Commission announced that 17.33 acres of the Griswoldville battlefield had been purchased and transferred to the Parks and Historic Sites Division of the Georgia Department of Natural Resources. The battle site was duly dedicated on November 21, 1998. Located on the ridge where the Federal troops dug in, the unmanned facility features a small parking area provided with a panel exhibit and two historical markers. The more elaborate of the markers includes a metal map affixed to the angled top of a concrete slab overlooking the battlefield (*Macon Telegraph*, 6 July 1997, pp. 1-2B; *Atlanta Journal-Constitution*, 22 November 1998, p. D7).

# *Selected Sources*

*Primary Sources*

I. Government Documents

A. US Government Documents, Printed and Manuscript

*Compiled Service Records of Confederate Soldiers Who Served in Organizations from the State of Georgia*, National Archives Microfilm Publication Microcopy No. 266.

Kennedy, Joseph C. G., ed. *Population of the United States in 1860*. Washington, DC, 1864.

National Archives Microfilm Publications. *Confederate Papers Relating to Citizens or Business Firms*, No. 346, Roll 383. Washington, DC, 1961.

————. *Records of Ordnance Establishments at Macon, Georgia*, No. NNO781, Reel 9. Washington, DC, 1971.

US Census Office. Manuscript 1850 Census, Slave Schedules, Jones County, Georgia (microfilm).

————. Manuscript 1860 Census of Population, Jones County, Georgia (microfilm).

————. Manuscript 1860 Census, Slave Schedules, Jones County, Georgia (microfilm).

US War Department. *War of the Rebellion: A Compilation of the Official Records of the Union and Confederate Armies*, 128 volumes. Washington, DC, 1880-1901.


B. State of Georgia Documents, Printed and Manuscript

Adjutant General's Office. Letter Book B-44. 2 volumes. Georgia Department of Archives and History, Atlanta GA.

————. Book of Commissions. Volume B-49, 1861-1865. Georgia Department of Archives and History, Atlanta GA.

*Annual Report of the Adjutant and Inspector General of the State of Georgia*. Milledgeville GA, 1864.

Candler, Allen D., ed. *The Confederate Records of the State of Georgia*. 5 volumes. Atlanta GA, 1909-1911.

*Governor Brown's Proclamations and Orders Calling into Active Military Service and Sending to the Front the Civil and Military Officers, and the Reserved Militia of the State of Georgia, to the Army of Tennessee*. Milledgeville GA, 1864.

Henderson, Lillian, compiler. *Roster of the Confederate Soldiers of Georgia*. 6 volumes. Hapeville GA, 1959-1964.

*Reports of the Operations of the Militia, from October 13, 1864, to February 11, 1865, by Maj.-Generals G. W. Smith and Wayne, together with Memoranda by Gen. Smith, for the Improvement of the State Military Organization*. Macon GA, 1865.

Statistical Reports of the First Division, Georgia Militia, 31 October and 10 November 1864, Georgia Department of Archives and History.


C. County Documents

"Beverly Daniel Evans," Book of Minutes 'H,' Folio 170, Washington County Courthouse, Sandersville GA.

County Affairs, 1842-1888, Probate Court, Jones County Courthouse, Gray, Georgia.

Deed Books, Office of the Clerk of the Superior Court, Jones County Courthouse, Gray GA.

Griswold, Samuel. Depredation Affidavit, 11 February 1865 (typescript in private possession).


II. Other Primary Sources

A. Correspondence and Reports

Boardman, Arthur E. Letter, 28 April 1929. Genealogical & Historical Room, Washington Memorial Library, Macon GA.

Brown, Joseph E., to P. G. T. Beauregard, 8 April 1865, Joseph E. Brown Papers, Duke University Library, Durham NC.

Bush, Andrew, to Mary Bush, 20 December 1864, Andrew Bush File, Indiana State Library, Indianapolis, IN.

Cobb, Howell, to Charles C. Jones, Jr., [c. September 1867]. Charles C. Jones, Jr. Papers, Duke University Library, Durham NC.

Cobb, Howell, to his wife, 3 August 1864. Cobb Papers. Hargrett Library. University of Georgia Libraries, Athens GA.

Cobb, Mary Ann, to Mrs. Howell Cobb, 31 July 1864. Cobb Papers, Hargrett Library, University of Georgia Libraries, Athens GA.

Colcock, Charles Jones, to Charles Colcock Jones, Jr., 5 November 1867, Charles C. Jones, Jr., Papers, Duke University Library, Durham NC.

Griswold, Samuel, to Merrit Camp, 25 October 1854. Miscellaneous File #481, Georgia Department of Archives and History, Atlanta GA.

Jackson, George T., to Charles C. Jones, Jr., undated, Charles C. Jones, Jr., Papers, Duke University Library, Durham NC.

Johnson, Samuel Griswold, to Louisa Griswold, 12 May & 30 November 1861, United Daughters of the Confederacy, Georgia Division, Bound Typescripts (14 volumes.), Georgia Department of Archives and History, Atlanta GA.

Lane, Mills, ed. *"Dear Mother: Don't grieve about me. If I get killed, I'll only be dead": Letters from Georgia Soldiers in the Civil War.* Savannah GA, 1977.

Lee, G. W. "Official Report of the Battle of East Macon, 30 July 1864," 4 August 1864, Cobb Papers, Hargrett Library, University of Georgia Libraries, Athens GA.

Philips, P. J., Correspondence File, Georgia Department of Archives and History, Atlanta GA.

Phillips, U. B., ed. *The Correspondence of Robert Toombs, Alexander H. Stephens, and Howell Cobb.* Washington, DC, 1913.

Stoneman, George, to his wife (telegram), 1 August 1864. William T. Sherman Papers, Volume 14, p. 1882, Library of Congress.


B. Memoirs, Unit Histories, Journals, and Diaries

Adamson, A. P. *Brief History of the Thirtieth Georgia Regiment.* Griffin GA, 1912.

Andrews, Eliza Frances. "A Visit to Clinton." *Jones County News,* 18 April 1901.

Arndt, A. F. R. *Reminiscences of an Artillery Officer.* Detroit MI, 1890.

Biddle, Ellen McGowan. *Reminiscences of a Soldier's Life.* Philadelphia PA, 1907.

Conyngham, David P. *Sherman's March Through the South.* New York, 1865.

Cornwell, Louise Caroline Reese. "A Paper Written and read…in the late Sixties." *Confederate Diaries*. Volume 5 (UDC, 1940) [Georgia Department of Archives and History].

Cox, Jacob Dolson. *Military Reminiscences of the Civil War*. 2 volumes. New York, 1900.

Dodson, W. C. "Stampede of Federal Cavalry." *Confederate Veteran* 19 (March 1911): 123-24.

Dodson, W. C., ed. *Campaigns of Wheeler and His Cavalry*. Atlanta GA, 1899.

Emilio, Luis F. *History of the Fifty-fourth Regiment of Massachusetts Volunteer Infantry*. Boston MA, 1894.

Ferguson, Joseph. *Life-Struggles in Rebel Prisons*. Philadelphia PA, 1866.

Gay, Mary A. H. *Life in Dixie during the War*. Atlanta GA, 1897.

Graham, Stephen. "Marching Through Georgia." *Harper's Monthly Magazine* 140 (April, May 1920): 612-20, 813-23.

Griswold, S. H. "Benjamin James, His Sons, and What They Accomplished." *Jones County News*, 15 April 1909.

———. "The Cotton Gin." *Jones County News*, 2 April 1908.

———. "Courage and Patriotism of Our Ancestors." *Jones County News*, 18 March 1909.

———. "A Little War History." *Jones County News*, 7 May 1908.

———. "The Old Way of Ginning." *Jones County News*, 10 June 1909.

———. "Passing of Stoneman's and Sherman's Armies." *Jones County News*, 19 November 1908.

———. "Pine Ridge Church in the Long Ago." *Jones County News*, 22 October 1908.

———. "Stoneman's Raid," *Jones County News*, 4 March 1909.

———. "Unwritten History. A Battle Fought in Jones County but Never Recorded." *Jones County News*, 3 July 1908.

Hardeman, Ellen Griswold. Manuscript Memoir of Samuel Griswold, in private possession.

Hargis, O. P. *Thrilling Experiences of a First Georgia Cavalryman in the Civil War*. Rome GA, n.d.

Harwell, Richard, ed. *Kate: The Journal of a Confederate Nurse*. Baton Rouge LA, 1959.

Hazen, W. B. *A Narrative of Military Service*. Boston MA, 1885.

Hinman, Wilbur F. *The Story of the Sherman Brigade*. Alliance OH, 1897.

Hitchcock, Henry. *Marching with Sherman*. New Haven CT, 1927.

Howard, Oliver Otis. *Autobiography of Oliver Otis Howard, Major General, United States Army*. 2 volumes. New York, 1907.

Isham, Asa B., et al. *Prisoners of War and Military Prisons*. Cincinnati OH, 1890.

Jackson, A. J. "Diary of the War Between the States kept by A. J. Jackson, Company G, Georgia State Line Troops, from February, 1863, to April, 1865 [Manuscript]." Microfilm Box 76-7, Georgia Department of Archives and History, Atlanta GA.

Johnson, Robert Underwood, and Clarence Clough Buel, eds. *Battles and Leaders of the Civil War*, 4 volumes. New York, 1887-1888.

Johnston, Joseph E. *Narrative of Military Operations*. New York, 1874.

Kerksis, Sidney C., ed. *The Atlanta Papers*. Dayton OH, 1980.

Kingman, Robert H., Sr. Deposition in *Reminiscences of Confederate Soldiers*, Volume

XII. UDC, 1940. Georgia Department of Archives and History, Atlanta GA.

McClary, Ben H., and LeRoy P. Graf, eds. "'Vineland' in Tennessee, 1852: The Journal of Rosine Parmentier," *The East Tennessee Historical Society's Publications* No. 31 (1959): 95-111.

Mallet, J. W. "Memoranda of my life—for my children." Accession No. 20. University of Virginia Library, Charlottesville VA.

Moore, Frank, ed. *The Rebellion Record.* 11 volumes. New York, 1861-1868.

Moore, James. *Kilpatrick and Our Cavalry.* New York, 1865.

Nichols, George Ward. *The Story of the Great March.* New York, 1865.

*Ninety-second Illinois Volunteers.* Freeport IL, 1875.

Nisbet, James Cooper. *Four Years on the Firing Line.* Edited by Bell I. Wiley. Jackson TN, 1963.

Pepper, George W. *Personal Recollections of Sherman's Campaigns in Georgia and the Carolinas.* Zanesville OH, 1866.

Platter, Cornelius C. Civil War Diary, 1864-1865 (Manuscript), Hargrett Rare Book and Manuscript Library, University of Georgia Libraries, Athens GA.

Ray, Ruby Felder ed. *Letters and Diary of Lieut. Lavender R. Ray, 1861-1865.* n.p., 1949.

*Reminiscences of the Civil War from Diaries of Members of the 103d Illinois Volunteer Infantry.* Chicago IL, 1904.

Robertson, John, compiler. *Michigan in the War.* Lansing MI, 1882.

Sanford, Washington L. *History of the Fourteenth Illinois Cavalry.* Chicago IL, 1898.

Sherlock, Eli J. *Memorabilia of the Marches and Battles in Which the One Hundredth Regiment of Indiana Volunteers Took an Active Part.* Kansas City MO, 1896.

Sherman, William T. *Memoirs of Gen. W. T. Sherman.* 2 volumes. New York, 1891.

Stewart, Thomas Jefferson. Diary, 1860. Georgia Department of Archives and History, Atlanta GA.

Tarrant, Eastham. *The Wild Riders of the First Kentucky Cavalry.* Louisville KY, 1894.

Taylor, Richard. *Destruction and Reconstruction.* New York, 1879.

Upson, Theodore F. *With Sherman to the Sea.* Baton Rouge LA, 1943.

Watkins, Sam R. *"Co. Aytch."* Chattanooga TN, 1900.

Wells, James M. *"With Touch of Elbow."* Philadelphia PA, 1909.

Wills, Charles W. *Army Life of an Illinois Soldier.* Washington, DC, 1906.

Wilson, James Harrison. *Under the Old Flag.* 2 volumes. New York, 1912.

Wynn, J. A. "Memoir." In *Confederate Diaries.* Volume 5. UDC, 1940. Georgia Department of Archives and History, Atlanta GA.


C. Newspapers

*Atlanta* (GA) *Daily Intelligencer.*
*Augusta* (GA) *Chronicle & Sentinel.*
*Christian Index.*
*Columbus* (GA) *Daily Enquirer-Sun.*
*Columbus* (GA) *Daily Sun.*
*Confederate Union* (Milledgeville GA).
*De Bow's Review.*
*Georgia Journal* (Milledgeville GA).

*Georgia Journal and Messenger* (Macon GA).

*Jones County* (GA) *News.*

*Macon* (GA) *Telegraph.*

*Southern Recorder* (Milledgeville GA).

*Southern Watchman* (Athens GA).


D. Miscellany

Atwater, Dorence. *A List of the Union Soldiers Buried at Andersonville.* New York, 1866.

*Grier's Southern Almanac.* Augusta GA, 1864.

Harwell, Richard Barksdale, ed., *Songs of the Confederacy.* New York, 1951.

Lewis, David W. *Transactions of the Southern Central Agricultural Society.* Macon GA, 1852.

*Lloyd's Southern Railroad Guide.* Atlanta GA, [1864].

*Reports of the Presidents and Superintendents of the Central Railroad and Banking Company of Georgia, from No. 20 to 32 Inclusive.* Savannah GA, 1868.

Schwaab, Augustus. *Diagram of Central RR Showing Location of Depots, Bridges, Buildings, Etc.,* Book 1 (1866). #1362FA-90/42-D-3, Georgia Historical Society, Savannah GA.

"To the Citizens of Macon...." (Macon GA, 1864). Broadside. Hargett Library, University of Georgia Libraries, Athens, GA.


*Secondary Sources*

Albaugh, William A., III. *The Confederate Brass-Framed Colt and Whitney.* Falls Church VA, 1955.

————. *Confederate Edged Weapons.* New York, 1960.

———— and Edward N. Simmons. *Confederate Arms.* Harrisburg PA, 1957.

————, et al., *Confederate Handguns.* Philadelphia PA, 1967.

Avery, Isaac W. *History of the State Of Georgia.* New York, 1881.

Bass, James Horace. "Georgia in the Confederacy, 1861-1865." Ph.D. dissertation, University of Texas, 1932.

Bennett, Charles A. *Saw and Toothed Cotton Ginning Developments.* Dallas, Texas, ca. 1960.

Bonner, James C. *Milledgeville: Georgia's Antebellum Capital.* Athens GA, 1978.

Bragg, William Harris. "The Fight at Honey Hill," 22 *Civil War Times Illustrated* (January 1984): 12-19.

————. "Howell Cobb's Account." *Civil War Times Illustrated* 20 (August 1981): 28-33.

————. "Joe Brown vs. the Confederacy." *Civil War Times Illustrated* 26 (November 1987): 40-43.

————. *Joe Brown's Army.* Macon GA, 1987.

————. "A Little Battle at Griswoldville." *Civil War Times Illustrated* 19 (November 1980): 44-49.

————. "The Union General Lost in Georgia." *Civil War Times Illustrated* 24 (June 1985): 16-23.

Britton, Karen Gerhardt. *Bale o' Cotton: The Mechanical Art of Cotton Ginning.* College Station TX, 1992.

Brockman, Charles J., Jr. "The Confederate Armory of Cook and Brother" *Papers of the Athens Historical Society* 2 (1979): 76-87.

———. "Life in Confederate Athens, Georgia." *Georgia Review* 21 (Spring 1967): 107-125.

Brown, Rodney Hilton. *American Polearms.* New Milford CT, 1967.

Brundage, Lyle D. "The Organization, Administration, and Training of the United States Ordinary and Volunteer Militia, 1792-1861." Ed.D dissertation, University of Michigan, 1958.

Butler, John C. *Historical Record of Macon and Central Georgia.* Macon GA, 1879.

Calhoun, Charles H., Sr. *Dr. Lindsey Durham: A Brief Biography; "The Durham Doctors": Biographical Sketches.* n.p., 1965.

Candler, Allen D. and Clement A. Evans, eds. *Georgia.* 3 volumes. Atlanta GA, 1906

Castel, Albert. *Decision in the West: The Atlanta Campaign of 1864.* Lawrence KS, 1992.

Cawthon, William Lamar, Jr. "Clinton: County Seat on the Georgia Frontier, 1808-1821." M.A. thesis, University of Georgia, 1984.

Colcock, Charles J., Jr. "The Battle of Honey Hill." Charleston SC, *Sunday News,* 10 December 1899.

Coleman, Kenneth, and Charles Stephen Gurr, eds. *Dictionary of Georgia Biography.* 2 volumes. Athens GA, 1983.

Cox, Jacob D. *The March to the Sea—Franklin and Nashville.* New York, 1882.

Cullum, George W. *Biographical Register of the Officers and Graduates of the US Military Academy.* 2 volumes. Boston MA, 1891.

Davis, Burke. *Sherman's March.* New York, 1980.

Derry, Joseph T. "A Condensed History." *Eighth Annual Report of the Commissioner of Commerce and Labor of the State of Georgia.* Atlanta GA, 1929.

———. *Georgia.* Volume 6 of *Confederate Military History.* 12 volumes. Atlanta GA, 1899.

Evans, David. *Sherman's Horsemen: Union Cavalry Operations in the Atlanta Campaign.* Bloomington IN, 1996.

Faust, Patricia L., ed. *Historical Times Illustrated Encyclopedia of the Civil War.* New York, 1986.

Fellman, Michael. *Citizen Sherman.* New York, 1995.

Foote, Shelby. *The Civil War: A Narrative.* 3 volumes. New York, 1958-1974.

Freeman, Douglas Southall. *Lee's Lieutenants.* 3 volumes. New York, 1942-1944

Futch, Ovid L. *History of Andersonville Prison.* Gainesville FL, 1968.

Gary, William A. *Confederate Revolvers.* Dallas TX, 1987.

Gunnison, George W. *A Genealogy of the Descendants of Hugh Gunnison.* Boston MA, 1880.

Hallock, Judith Lee. "Braxton Bragg and Confederate Defeat." Ph.D. dissertation, State University of New York at Stony Brook, 1989.

Hesseltine, William Best. *Civil War Prisons.* Columbus OH, 1930.

Hill, Louise Biles. *Joseph E. Brown and the Confederacy.* Chapel Hill NC, 1939.

Hull, A. L. *The Campaigns of the Confederate Army.* Atlanta GA, 1901.

Hutchings, Richard Henry. *Hutchings, Bonner, Wyatt: An Intimate Family History.* Utica NY, 1937.

Irvine, Dallas D. *Military Operations of the Civil War, A Guide-Index to the Official Records.* 5 volumes. Washington, DC, 1966-1980/US National Archives Microfilm M1036.

Jones, Charles C., Jr. *The Siege of Savannah in December, 1864.* Albany NY, 1874.

Jones, James Pickett. *Yankee Blitzkrieg.* Athens GA, 1976.

Jones, Mary Callaway. *Some Historic Spots of the Confederacy Period in Macon.* Macon GA, 1937.

Jones, Mary G., and Lily Reynolds, eds. *Coweta County Chronicles.* Atlanta GA, 1928.

Kurtz, Wilbur G. "Whitehall Tavern." *The Atlanta Historical Bulletin* (April 1931): 42-49.

Lawrence, Alexander A. "Henry Kent McCay—Forgotten Jurist." *Georgia Bar Journal.* 9 (August 1946): 5-29.

————. *A Present for Mr. Lincoln.* Macon GA, 1961.

Lenz, Richard J. *The Civil War in Georgia: An Illustrated Traveler's Guide.* Watkinsville GA, 1995.

Liddell Hart, B. H. *Sherman: Soldier, Realist, American.* New York, 1929.

McInvale, Morton R. "'All That Devils Could Wish For': The Griswoldville Campaign." *Georgia Historical Quarterly* 60 (Summer 1976): 117-30.

————. "'That Thing of Infamy,' Macon's Camp Oglethorpe during the Civil War." *Georgia Historical Quarterly* 63 (Summer 1979): 279-91.

Mahon, John K. *History of the Militia and the National Guard.* New York, 1983.

Martin, John H. *Columbus, Georgia: 1827-1865.* 2 volumes. Columbus GA, 1874-1875.

Marvel, William. *Andersonville: The Last Depot.* Chapel Hill NC, 1994.

Middle Georgia Historical Society. *Macon…An Architectural & Historical Guide.* Macon GA, 1996.

Montgomery, Horace. *Howell Cobb's Confederate Career.* Tuscaloosa AL, 1959.

Moore, Albert Burton. *Conscription and Conflict in the Confederacy.* New York, 1924.

Old Clinton Historical Society. *An Historical Guide to Clinton, Georgia, An Early Nineteenth Century County Seat.* n.p., 1975.

Parks, Joseph H. *Joseph E. Brown of Georgia.* Baton Rouge LA, 1977.

Phillips, U. B. *A History of Transportation in the Eastern Cotton Belt to 1860.* New York, 1908.

Pratt, Merrill E. *Daniel Pratt: Alabama's First Industrialist.* Birmingham AL, 1949.

Scaife, William R. *The Campaign for Atlanta.* Saline MI, 1985.

————. *The March to the Sea.* Saline MI, 1993.

————. "Sherman's March to the Sea." *Blue & Gray Magazine* 7 (December 1989): 10-32, 38-42.

Smedlund, William S. *Camp Fires of Georgia's Troops, 1861-1865.* Sharpsburg GA, 1994.

Starr, Stephen Z. *The Union Cavalry in the Civil War.* 3 volumes. Baton Rouge LA, 1979-1985.

Stearns, Ezra S., compiler. *Genealogical and Family History of the State of New Hampshire.* 4 volumes. New York, 1908.

Stovall, Pleasant A. *Robert Toombs.* New York, 1892.

Sword, Wiley. *Firepower from Abroad: The Confederate Enfield and the Le Mat Revolver, 1861-1863 with New Data on a Variety of Confederate Small Arms.* Lincoln RI, 1986.

Tarrant, Mrs. S. F. H., ed. *Hon. Daniel Pratt: A Biography.* Richmond VA, 1904.

Tweedale, Geoffrey. *Sheffield Steel and America: A Century of Commercial and Technological Interdependence, 1830-1930.* Cambridge MA, 1987.

Wagener, Jane McIntosh. "General Kilpatrick's Cavalry in Sherman's March to the Sea." M.A. thesis, University of Georgia, 1957.

Warner, Ezra J. *Generals in Blue.* Baton Rouge LA, 1964.

————. *Generals in Gray.* Baton Rouge LA, 1959.

Watkins, James L. *King Cotton: A Historical and Statistical Review, 1790-1908.* New York, 1908.

Wells, Charles F. *The Battle of Griswoldville: 'Georgia's Gettysburg,' November 21-22, 1864.* Macon GA, 1961.

Welsh, Jack D. *Medical Histories of Union Generals.* Kent OH, 1996.

White, George. *Statistics of the State of Georgia.* Savannah GA, 1849.

Williams, Carolyn White. *History of Jones County, Georgia.* Macon GA, 1957.

Wolff, Lynn E. *Old Clinton Cemetery.* n.p., 1978.

Wright, Henry H. *A History of the Sixth Iowa Infantry.* Iowa City IA, 1923.

Young, Bennett H. *Confederate Wizards of the Saddle.* Boston MA, 1914.

# Afterword And Acknowledgments

In checking back for the date of origin of *Griswoldville*, I was surprised to find that I had written the first version in late 1977. This suggests that, with the present incarnation, the piece has finally reached its majority (though perhaps not full maturity and certainly not a definitive state). It was originally prepared to fulfill one of the requirements of a graduate class at Georgia College at Milledgeville, "Historical Methods and Interpretation" taught—fortunately for me—by the legendary William Ivy Hair.

The paper marked the first time that I committed an act of historiography, and I vividly remember the excitement of doing the research for it. Exploring the battlefield and its environs with Charles F. Wells was a revelation; I was very fortunate to have the benefit of his lifetime of interest in the Griswoldville area and the battle fought there, and I am glad that I thought to make a typescript of my interview with him, which he supplied with manuscript corrections and additions.

Book and manuscript research took me for the first time to the three principal meccas of the Georgia historian, where heady experiences awaited: the Georgia Department of Archives and History and the libraries of Emory University and the University of Georgia. At all three I accumulated many debts to many devoted archivists and librarians.

Since the original version of this story appeared so long ago, and since over the years there have been several revisions and transformations (including a curious typescript titled "Harvest of Death," which was distributed in fewer than six anonymous copies and took on a life of its own), I have become indebted to many people—too numerous to record—who have helped me with corrections and additions as each new version was prepared. I am very grateful to them all and regret that space does not allow me to thank them individually, as they deserve.

I must, however, express my thanks here to a number of people whose contributions have been extraordinary: Carolyn White Williams, whose wonderful history of Jones County remains the first stop for anyone interested in the county's past; Bill Moffat, always prodigal in sharing many of his historical discoveries and his insights—relating to Griswoldville and otherwise; Laura Nelle O'Callaghan, for her preservation and sharing of manuscript and photographic materials relating to her Griswold ancestors; Bill Scaife, for his expertise and assistance on matters relating to Georgia in the war, always so cordially given; Bud Merritt, master of battlefield archeology and acknowledged expert on what happened at Griswoldville; Howard Childs, Mac Davis, and Donald Phillips for vital assistance at Stoneman's Hill and Duncan's Farm; Willard Rocker of the Genealogical and Historical Room of Washington Memorial Library, who has long supplied researchers with his expert knowledge of that facility's holdings—with infinite patience and a side order of good humor; Bill Cawthon, who gave this manuscript a close reading and made several important corrections and valuable suggestions; Anne Hamilton, mainstay of the Old Clinton Historical Society, and the society's members, past and present, for working so long and tirelessly to preserve Clinton for posterity (and, for unselfishly helping them in this effort, the several re-enactment units—principally, Company G, 16th Georgia—that bring to life both Griswoldville and Sunshine Church at the annual Old Clinton War Days); David Evans, chronicler of the Union cavalry in the Atlanta Campaign, who shared with me an invaluable copy of a long-lost map; Mary Ellen Brooks and Nelson Morgan, treasured allies at the Hargrett Rare Book and Manuscript Library, and the talented Sarah Lockmiller, who made many of the photographs for this book from the Hargrett's collections; E. P. Leftwich of Gunnison, Mississippi, who graciously provided Gunnison lore and saw to it personally that Arvin Nye Gunnison's photograph illustrated this book; and David Wynn Vaughan, who kindly allowed me to print several previously unpublished images from his superlative personal archive.

My thanks are also due to all those people and facilities whose names appear in the credits for the illustrations and in the bibliography, but I must mention especially for their courtesy Gordon L. Jones, Curator of Military History, Atlanta History Center; William A. Gary; Gary L. Kross; Dr. R. Stuart Lester; and, in Adrian, Michigan, Suzanne Wayda-Slomski and Charles Linquist.

My greatest debt of gratitude is the closest to home—in the home, actually. In the two-score-plus years since I wrote the college paper on Griswoldville, other articles and books have followed, all traceable back to it in one way or another. The vital constant in researching them, writing them, and preparing them for publication has been my wife, Wanda: ever-helpful, ever-tolerant, cheerful in all weathers.

# Index

Note: Italicized numbers indicate images of the subjects.

## A

Academy Hospital, Macon 56
Adams, George W. 48
Adams, Col. Silas *28*, 30, 33, 39, 56, 70, 73, 74
Allen, Brig. Gen. W. W. 67, *69*
Americus, Georgia 172n.155
Anderson, Brig. Gen. Charles D. *128*, 130, 140
Anderson, Capt. Ruel W. *119*, 121, 122, 130, 139
Andersonville, Georgia 30, 64, 82, 166n.83
Arndt, Capt. A.F.R. *115*, 130, 134
"Arp, Bill" (Charles Henry Smith) 48
Athens, Georgia 74, 122
Athens and Augusta Battalions 130, 134, 137, 151, 152, 171n.144
Atlanta, Georgia 67, 85, 86, 90, 167n.91, 172n.158
Atlanta Wright Guards 48
Atwood, Berry 74
Augusta, Georgia 89, 90

## B

Baldwin, Pvt. S. J. *12*
Barfield, John 67
Barfield plantation 67, *76*
Barron, William Wiley 36
Barron plantation 36
"Battleline Branch" 116
Bear Creek Station, Georgia 91
"Bear's Den," Macon *38*, 40
Beauregard, Gen. P. G. T. *147*, 166n.87, 168n.99
Biddle, Col. James *27*, 30, 39, 73, 165n.79
Blind School Hospital, Macon 100
Blount, Thomas 4
Blount plantation 36
Blountsville, Georgia 92
Bonner, Ellen Griswold 12

Bonner, Richard Wyatt, 12, 155
Bonner family 12
Bonner residence, Clinton 12, 39
Bonner's Hill 96
Boren, Lt. Lewis W. *32*
Bowen plantation 36
Breckinridge, Col. W. C. P. 67, 72, 74, 110
"Brick House" *2, 3, 7*
Brown, Dwight 7
Brown, Israel 7
Brown, Joseph E. 16, 40, 41, 44, 48, 91, 103, 109, 129, 150, 153, 167n.91, 173n.166
Burton, Col. James H. 123

## C

Camp Griswold, Griswoldville 16
Camp Oglethorpe, Macon *25*, 30, 56, 82, 152
Camp Sumter, Andersonville 30, 166n.83
Camp Wayne, Griswoldville 16
"Cannonball House," Macon *59*
Capron, Col. Horace *26*, 30, 39, 51, 52, 70, 74
Carswell, Brig. Gen. Reuben W. 110, 150, 151, 152, 173n.169
Catterson, Col. Robert F. *112*, 139, 140
Central of Georgia Railroad 9, 51, 110
Chancellorsville, Virginia 19, 30
Chattanooga, Tennessee 29
Christ Church (Episcopal), Macon 85
Clinton, Georgia 3, 4, 9, 15, 19, 33, *34-35*, 64, 92, 95, 99, 152, 173n.167
Cobb, Maj. Gen. Howell *37*, 40, 44, 48, 51, 56, 86, 91, 109, 152
Colcock, Col. Charles J. 152, 174n.170
Colcock, Charles J., Jr. 174n.170
Colmes, Col. Stephen H. 100
Columbus, Georgia 152
Confederate Armory, Macon 19, 44
Confederate Arsenal, Macon 19, 44
Confederate Central Laboratory, Macon 44, *53*
Confederate Medical Examining Board 16
Confederate Reserve Force 40, 44, 48, 89, 122, 163n.45, 173n.161
Confederate Thanksgiving 85